Praise for *Finding Li*

"Nordenson describes wrestling with work as with a large force that wants to have its way with you, even as you want to have your way with it. This wrestling, sinewy and particular as its wrestler, enlarges us as we read our way into her life with its incisive insights and explorations. Can one wrestle meditatively? This author has learned the art and we are the benefactors."

—Luci Shaw, writer in residence, Regent College; author,
Adventure of Ascent: Field Notes from a Lifelong Journey and *Scape: Poems*

"Written with a rare wit and elegance, *Finding Livelihood* offers a profound, often surprising reflection on the necessity of earning our daily bread. This fine new collection by Nancy Nordenson, which gathers under one cover such unlikely bedfellows as venipuncture, a flute-playing cabbie, and the prudent way to unpack Russian icons, includes some of the best essays I've read in years."

—Paula Huston, author of *A Land Without Sin* and *The Holy Way*

"This is an absolutely timely book, and an absolutely beautiful one too. Ms. Nordenson examines what it means to work, and does so in a lyrical, practical, moving, and spirit-filled way. In giving us her personal stories and universal observations, we are given as well the means by which, in these difficult days, to make sense of what it means *to work*. I like this book a lot for its voice and vision, and especially for its hope."

—Bret Lott, author of *Letters and Life: On Being a Writer,
On Being a Christian* and *Jewel*

"In this extraordinary new book, Nordenson asks what we all want to know: Can our daily workplace grind really become our daily God-blessed bread? (My personal question: Can cleaning fishing nets of rotting jellyfish really be redeeming work?) Nancy answers an unequivocal 'yes'! Through layered eloquent prose and her own vast experience, she offers us real ways of finding astonishment and transcendence even in the most stultifying jobs. This book is a revelation. It goes with me to my fishing camp."

—Leslie Leyland Fields, author *Surviving the Island of Grace* and *Forgiving Our Fathers and Mothers*; contributing editor, *Christianity Today*

"*Finding Livelihood* is a breath of radical honesty for the workaday Christian. Nancy Nordenson does not fear the long dark night shift of the soul, but neither does she accept it. Her real world stories of people at work inspire and challenge at every turn.»

—Marcus Goodyear, Editor of *The High Calling*

"Nordenson's prose is beautifully polished, lucid, and imaginative."

—Gregory Wolfe, editor of *Image*, author of *Beauty Will Save The World*

"*Finding Livelihood* is deeply felt and deeply satisfying to the reader. Nordenson grapples with hard questions and avoids easy answers. Of work itself she writes: 'You take the first steps in a state of delight, equipped with skill or talent, ready to make a difference. But the path is never straight, and it takes you through places you never envisioned.' Nordenson's book is practical, powerful, and rooted in biblical wisdom and the wisest thought of the Western tradition. With a light step, and gratitude, Nordenson teaches us to deal with jagged changes and ugly surprises, 'to live and work in the flow of God's love.'"

—Emilie Griffin, author of *The Reflective Executive* and *Souls in Full Sail*

Finding Livelihood

A Progress of Work and Leisure

NANCY J. NORDENSON

Nancy J Nordenson

For Pam,
With gratitude for your
friendship and blessings on
your writing.
N—

www.kalospress org

Published by Kalos Press, a literary imprint of Doulos Resources
P.O. Box 69485, Oro Valley AZ 85737
901-201-4612 | www.kalospress.org

Cover and interior design by Valerie Anne Bost
Printed in the United States of America

Portions of this book first appeared in the following publications: "Still in French Airspace"
and "Witness" in *Under the Sun*, "Two-Part Invention" in *Harvard Divinity Bulletin*, "A Place at
the Table" in *Relief*, and "Spinning and Being Spun" in *Comment*.

Nancy J. Nordenson, "Two-Part Invention," *Harvard Divinity Bulletin*, Vol. 42, Nos. 3 and 4
(Summer/Autumn 2014): 28-33. Copyright 2014 The President and Fellows of Harvard
College. Reprinted with permission.

Nordenson, Nancy J., 1957–
   Finding livelihood: a progress of work and leisure / Nancy J. Nordenson.
   ISBNs: 978-1-937063-59-7 (Print), 978-1-937063-58-0 (Digital)

14 15 16 17 18 19 20 21   10 9 8 7 6 5 4 3 2 1

For my parents, Janet and John

What is a Progress but an account of a series of pitfalls and illuminations leading to Revelation?

—Fanny Howe, *Winter Sun: Notes on A Vocation*

Is there still an area of human action, or human existence as such, that does not have its justification by being part of the machinery of a "five-year plan?"

—Josef Pieper, *Leisure: The Basis of Culture*

Contents

ACT III

Prologue

WHAT THIS BOOK IS AND IS NOT

The publication of Studs Terkel's *Working: People Talk About What They Do All Day and How They Feel About What They Do* in the early 1970s gave the reading public eyes to see ordinary people at work. On his pages, readers met Heather Lamb, a telephone operator who confided, "It's a hard feeling when everyone's in a hurry to talk to somebody else, but not to talk to you." And Therese Carter, a housewife: "What I do is only important to five people." And Steve Dubi, a steelworker: "When your work sheet is sent in your name isn't put down, just your number." Terkel gave voices to more than 100 other men and women working at jobs ranging from airline stewardess to film critic to pharmacist.

I first dipped into *Working* when I was in high school. By then I had only worked assorted, sequential, part-time jobs, but the unknown future work world was an exciting hope. There would be college, a choice of major, a career, and off I'd go.

My first non-babysitting job came during my high school junior year. On a whim, I applied to be a hostess at a dinner theater in the neighborhood shopping mall and was hired for several evening or weekend shifts per week. My job description included showing guests to their reserved seats, serving soft drinks during the meal and intermissions, and changing the towel dispensers in the women's restroom. During the show, I was free to watch or to sit in the lounge area with the waitstaff, who doubled as a talented singing troupe that performed before the shows and during intermissions. On the stage were celebrities on a circuit: a former Miss America, former film stars and teen idols. The first week or so, I initially watched the show but then joined the waitstaff's huddle in the lounge and listened to conversations well beyond my age. In the weeks that followed, I moved to a separate table where I did my history, trigonometry, and anatomy and physiology homework.

For the singing troupe and celebrities, this theater, situated between a grocery store and a discount retail store, or places like it, was their livelihood; my future was somewhere else. In the introduction to *Working*, Terkel wrote that although the book is about work, "...it is about a search, too, for daily meaning as well as daily bread, for recognition as well as cash, for astonishment rather than torpor; in short, for a sort of life rather than a Monday through Friday sort of dying." I had every intention, while sitting at my homework table, that my future work would be satisfying and meaningful, but the conversations at the other table suggested that life takes unexpected turns.

I started writing this book after my husband lost his job shortly after I began graduate school to pursue what I felt was a call, a dream, a passion. I had hoped to drastically cut back my full-time workweek to give it my all. There was no easy solution when he came home with the news. We had two sons in college. A mortgage. My husband began the difficult task of looking for a job in his field, one in which he had felt a long-term call. I worked longer and harder to meet requirements of both school and job. In the prelude to and the wake of the 2008 economic crisis, his unemployment, like that of so many others, particularly men, became chronic underemployment.

This is not a book for the young girl at the table doing her homework and dreaming of the future. It is a book for when the future has arrived. It is not about choosing a career path but about making your way on a path that you have either chosen or been given.

In my adult life, I have worked part time and full time. I've taken maternity leaves for babies, brought children to daycare, negotiated longer days but shorter work weeks, negotiated a job share arrangement and an employer's first-ever telecommuting arrangement, started a sole proprietorship that failed and another that succeeded, and from time to time—although I'm not proud to admit it—paid my children to not interrupt me at the computer or during work calls unless one of them was bleeding.

While grateful, very grateful, for all the opportunities I have had to earn a living, I have also yawned in boredom or disinterest, cried in discouragement, fumed in anger, and kicked a door or two. I have been scolded by difficult bosses, felt sick to my stomach driving to work in the mornings, lain awake at night wondering if the debit and credit columns would add up, had pay freezes and work intensifications, been followed with a stopwatch for time-motion studies à la Frederick Taylor, seen merit raises abolished under the name of Deming's quality improvement, and been grief-stricken and afraid at my husband's loss of jobs. I have heard my friends' stories of harsh and unreasonable supervisors, threatening customers and clients, long hours, irresponsible co-workers, damaging management decisions, and financial stress—even ruin. No matter how carefully you choose your work path or cultivate that path with professional development and sweat, most jobs do not equate to ongoing passion and bliss. I have stared into the question, *Is this all there is?*

Like Terkel's workers, I too, now far from my high school daydreams about the future, am on a search for daily meaning as well as for daily bread, for living rather than dying. I want to cast my net on the side of astonishment, even though a workweek often tempts me toward torpor. I want to find God at work in me and through me. I want *livelihood.*

Livelihood: the word gathers up and bundles together the simultaneous longings for meaning, satisfaction, and provision. In the fullest sense of the word, livelihood means the way of one's life; it means the sustenance to make that way possible; it means both body and soul are fully alive thanks to what has been earned or received by grace. On one level we make our livelihood; on another level we keep our eyes open and find it.

My point of view has long been one of transcendence, and I'm hoping now that focus helps me make peace with work. I don't use transcendence to imply a pep-talk mentality or a message of conquest. Transcendence, instead, speaks to a quest. I'm on the lookout for signs of the transcendent, God-filled reality that buoys the universe and enfolds our quotidian activities in vital participation. Juxtapose this point of view with the nagging question, *Is this all there is?* and that's as good a definition of faith as I know.

This book admits that work, even good work for which we are grateful and love, has a shadow side. It is not about disengaging from unsatisfying work or finding a new job. Instead, this book is about developing openness to meaning and beholding meaning where you find it. This book is about watching for signs of transcendent reality and participating in that reality, even when work fails to satisfy. This book is about work—and it is about more than work.

Philosophers and theologians espouse theories of work: work as co-creation with God, work as call to a divinely ordained place, work as the means to leisure. These and other theories represent efforts to give work meaning or to underscore one's participation in life through work. Most people, however, carry out their work untouched by theory. We live in the physical world of desks and pens and cash registers, not in the pages of rhetorical abstractions. We are caught in work's daily grind, whether the venue is a downtown office or the neighborhood grocery store. The tasks build; chores swirl one into the other; labor falls heavy. Yet, life woos, life calls from beyond the canopy of work.

Expert voices easily address the never-ending search for job satisfaction with career advice from behind the lectern or multimedia presentation. They talk of passion and bliss, the chosen life, and aspirations achieved in 10 steps. Anything short of success by those standards and you are left to wonder, *Did I take a wrong turn?* From behind the pulpit, other voices paste spiritual lessons of victory on work's challenges, but things look different from the pews.

Even the often quoted and highly respected advice of theologian and writer Frederick Buechner is problematic: "the place God calls you to is the place where your deep gladness and the world's deep hunger meet." While Buechner's words, an amplification of a sentiment first voiced by Aristotle, offer a starting point for dreams and plans when the future is in front of you and the choice is yours, who but a very small minority can find that exact intersection and from it feed a family? Or at that sweet spot sustain their position for a lifetime? Glance at history or literature and count the heroes who are swept into events not of their choosing, sometimes kicking and screaming. Consider the pivotal, but sometimes hidden, events visited upon the common man or woman who work far from deep gladness, the world's greatest need, or both.

This book is not about the modern work ethic. It is not a celebration of work, but neither is it an exposé or complaint. This book is about wrestling with work as with any large and powerful force that wants to have its way with you while you simultaneously want to have your way with it. This book adds another view to the body of literature about work. It adds not just another way of thinking about the experience of work but another voice, a meditative and contemplative voice, a voice trying to speak into the tension between passion and need, between aspiration and limits, between the planned life and the given life.

~

The style of *Finding Livelihood* is lyric, which means there is a nonlinear structure, white space, metaphor, and slant-angle perspective. It is a way of exploring, not a way of explaining. Lyric structure bypasses the default problem-solving logic of self-help books and the chronologic reportage of memoir to more closely mimic the nature of a complex issue that can't be resolved in 10 easy steps but can be seen and understood in new ways when explored from multiple directions.

Lyric style finds clues and layers them or braids them together. It uses story, collage, and juxtaposition. It invites you to join your thought process to mine. It invites you to dwell on its pages, to enter the experience of contemplation. I wrote this book looking out from where I sit at my own work desk, but this book is not about me. Let the words and images spin you off into meditations of your own experiences of work.

Come along with me, and consider the journey that is livelihood.

ACT I

Where we encounter ground level and metaphysical realities;
unfair rules, job stress, and bad bosses; idealistic work experts
and criteria for "good work"; hiddenness and exhaustion;
and a longing for meaning and a will to be satisfied.

Jobs are not big enough for people. It's not just the assembly
line worker whose job is too small for his spirit, you know?

—Nora Watson, editor in Studs Terkel's, *Working*

ONE
Travels in Sunshine City

ON THE POINT OF LAUNCH

I live under the roar of airplanes. A flight path to the Minneapolis-St. Paul International Airport extends in a trajectory overhead. The planes are on their final descent. A Boeing 757 or Airbus 320 flying over my backyard passes northwest to southeast in the time it takes for me to say, "I wonder where they've been." Looking up, I can see a plane's underbelly, flat and smooth like a shark's. I can see its strand of windows and the logo on the fuselage or wing. I can see the plane's nose, where in the cockpit the pilot lowers and steers the body of aluminum and various composites, slicing through the sky. Then it's gone, toward the runway only minutes ahead. The engine rumble lingers, like the thunder that travels through space long after lightning flashes.

It is Holy Week.

I'm working against a deadline.

Today, I've moved my workstation from the desk to the porch because winter has become spring. I can do my day job anywhere, and so I do it everywhere and always. My clients' timing becomes my own.

I am a freelance medical writer. I write on medical topics for clients, converting case notes into teaching tools, bullet points into slides, and data into prose. Breath and blood, flesh and brain, heart and bones.

I am a "penman," an appellative earned by virtue of the word's second definition in the *Oxford English Dictionary*: a person skilled in writing. More often than not, I serve according to the parameters set forth in its first definition: a person employed to use the pen on behalf of someone else.

In front of me, I see on the computer screen a PowerPoint slide with a blue background and words in white Arial font—always Arial in 24 to 32 points—anchored by square gold bullets to match the slide title's gold Arial 40-point font. I estimate conservatively that 8,000 or more slides in this format have passed before my eyes in the last 15 years.

Lately, in lieu of working, I find myself doodling arcs: an upside down U, a mountain's silhouette, a long drawn-out frown, the arch of a brow, a standard bell-shaped curve. How steep shall I make the slope upward, how long the plateau forward, how gradual the descent? How shall I label the horizontal and the vertical axes? The arcs could signify a plane's flight, or maybe the shape of one's life with a single ascent toward living and living, perhaps with an apex, followed by one descent toward death, but neither of these explanations is on my mind as I move my pen left to right across the page. An X marks the point of launch.

My tool is wearing down with miles left to go. A number of the keys on this computer keyboard are nearly or completely bare:

A, B, C, E, F, L, M, N, and V. The black lettering has rubbed off by typing certain words so many times—my name with its five Ns, virus, cancer, liver, bone, blood, malignant, mL, hepatitis C—and the keyboard shortcuts for copy and paste, save and find. I punch the keys in a rush and the clicks send messages zigzagging around the labyrinth of wiring inside this rectangular box I cannot work—cannot live—without. When I look at the keys, disconnecting my actions from habit and touch to concentration on sight alone, my fingers slow and stumble, looking for markers. With so many letters rubbed off, I work best on autopilot. My fingers move where they've known to move before. I've heard it said that people do what they do because they can't think of alternatives, but viable alternatives are hard to come by. Winds of recession or depression have been blowing through these streets, and no mark of Passover exemption has been made on my doorpost.

A couple of months earlier, my husband had arrived home from work, hours late, and stood in the doorway of our kitchen, dark but for a dim light over the sink. He told me his job was gone. No warning. Only the day before, his boss had told him, You're doing great, no worries. Yet there he stood, holding his box of personal belongings from his desk: a framed picture of me, another of our sons, a mug, his calendar.

It is Holy Week. These days, more than any others, ask that the ordinary yield to the extraordinary, but how is it possible?

I'm working against a deadline.

In the visual field dancing along and past the white plastic border of my laptop, my neighbor Bob, a retired electrician, is working in his yard. He kneels on the ground from which hosta will emerge in a few weeks alongside his house. He is clearing out the clutter that the melted snow revealed. He is tan and fit in his jeans and gray T-shirt. Handful by handful he removes the dead leaves and debris and places it all in a plastic bag. The bag's top ripples in the breeze. Bob, in his eighth decade, easily rises and kneels again before a spirea bush, repeating the cleansing ritual.

Other visual fields call. Like a choir with a missing member or a cityscape absent a tower, the neighborhood's arboreal skyline from this vantage point at my computer has a space where an oak tree recently stood. The mighty oak dated back to when this city land had been farmland. My husband and I saw what happened, sitting outside on a sunny and still day. Witnessing doesn't prove causality, but how could we not have a strong suspicion? Whether an intuitive sense or the rumble of subliminal thunder prompted us, we turned our heads at the right second. The puff, the swoosh, the bursting current lasted about a second, the time it takes to blow out a candle. If we had been distracted by so much as a mosquito on the arm or a ball rolling into the yard or tipping back our cups for the last drop of coffee, we would have missed it. A wind—was it wind?—pierced the canopy of the old tree, back to front.

I once heard a man on television say that we were on the verge of discovering parallel realities right where we live. A locomotive could be passing through us here and now, he had said. I was a young girl then and his words stopped me in my tracks. I tried to imagine standing against the rush of an invisible train. *What's really going on here?* That question stays with me.

The tree's limbs parted like the Red Sea, and a hole opened up big enough for a car to drive through, the leaves shivering on the fringe. Then it was over. The limbs hurried back in place, and the afternoon went on, sunny and still. The oak stood in its hard-wood glory throughout that summer. In fall, its leaves changed color on schedule, then dropped as expected at the threshold of winter. By the next spring, the tree was dead. Its limbs, dark and empty, silhouetted against the sky. Later that summer a truck arrived, and men hung on belts from branches, chain sawing it down piece by piece.

In front of me is the work, and side-by-side are questions that summon like a pair of unseen eyes you sense are looking your way. I want work to be smooth sailing, and it sometimes is, but I learn little from those times I whistle or dance in my office. My mind whirls with questions asked and answered only when I'm pushing against something that's pushing back. A hidden reality rises up and says, *Deal with me,* like something encountered only because I tripped over it in the dark.

I want to know, What meaning can be claimed on the shadow side of work where rules of the game don't feel fair? In what other economy can work gain purchase? For what other arcs of progress is work a point of launch? *What's really going on here?*

Bob's attention will soon turn to his roses. The two trellises of violet clematis. The hyacinth and lilacs. The peonies. When the maple tree launches its whirlybird seeds later this season, he will pluck them up one by one, again on his knees. Sometimes he sits on a lawn chair and reaches to suck them up with a vacuum. The whirlybirds that cross our yard line get no such special treatment but take their chances with the breeze, the thatch, and the lawn mower. Bob looks across at our lawn and sees bare spots, the re-sidual effects of a dog and two boys. "Don't worry," he once told my husband, "the kids are more important." He has no view here of flowering trellises, and our uncultivated ground offers no hope of return on the tomatoes and cucumbers he has grown and left at our back door for years.

Here in this neighborhood, in this area under the curve, in this city just beyond the reach of the Great Plains, in this mysterious metaphysical God-filled universe is where I live and work. Here, I find my livelihood, even while I am making it.

Engines thrust forward and in a matter of seconds, I lose my bearings. Whenever I'm on board a plane, seated and taking off, the wide-angle, top-down view of where I live never fails to disorient me, so at odds it is with the view up close and from below. The urge to find familiar markers comes fresh with every flight: the river, the mall, the stadium, the helicopter pad on the hospital where I used to work, a stretch of highway with its Celtic knot exchange, the chain of lakes. Like a game, look fast. The plane, while facilitator of the view, is also my opponent. It banks before my eyes can travel far enough or focus. I may or may not find my way before the rate of ascent overtakes my ability to see the familiar with clarity. If I were to keep ascending while the world kept turning, I'd see the curve of the horizon with cities, towns, and neighborhoods stretching from Pacific to Atlantic and back again.

Holy Week edges toward Good Friday, and at the grocery store down the street, the food was heaped in glorious display: asparagus, broccoli, celery, Red Delicious and Granny Smith apples, potatoes for scalloping and mashing, hams, and turkeys. My grocery list stated needs, but how I long for something more than necessity to seduce me. Hot cross buns and marshmallow chicks;

white lilies and fuchsia azaleas; cinnamon and cloves. Someone has placed mounds of green, yellow, and blue plastic grass along the inside of the deli counter with two pastel-dyed eggs in every third mound, perhaps the woman who sliced the smoked turkey for me, thin for sandwiches.

At the bank, the teller joked with the man at her window as she cashed his check. She fake-ordered him, "Now get out" when their transaction concluded. This teller knows her customers by name. Every month she sends thank-you letters to 40 military men and women serving overseas, different people each month, none of whom she knows. She tells me about this when I come to make a deposit or withdrawal. Once, she slid a letter across the counter for me to read. A soldier to whom she had written took the time to write her, and she was all smiles. Today, she wore new glasses with purple frames. At my turn, she deposited my paycheck, and we tried to find something funny about it all going back out in taxes in a few days.

Outside, a man who works in the bank stood near the door and smoked a cigarette in the sunshine. He nodded as I walked past. I looked through the window of the adjacent coffee shop. A barista steamed milk behind the counter, and a small crowd of people sat at tables with their laptops open. Just beyond the intersection, a mason wearing all white—cap, T-shirt, and painter's pants—repaired a collapsed retaining wall along the sidewalk. He had already swept the original crumbled stone to the side. Bending over, he spread wet cement then smoothed it. Spread, then smoothed.

"Sunshine City" was the name—as I remember it—that my seventh-grade social studies teacher gave to a special two-week unit. When she called it a game, we thought it would be fun. She was fun.

Between classes, Mrs. D would stand at the intersection of the two perpendicular hallways just before the stairwell and joke with students as they passed, her hair a bouffant of blond teased curls. Her classroom had pale green walls with a bank of windows to our left as we were seated at wood desks. Mrs. D's desk and blackboard were at the front. My good friend Susan and I sat next to each other, one row back from the front and a couple rows over from the window.

Earlier there had been the lesson on opposable thumbs. Tape your thumbs tight against your hands and find out how hard it is to grab the paper Mrs. D hands to you, the paper she hovers high above your head, or to unwrap your sandwich at lunch. Go through an hour or a day blindfolded and appreciate the ability to see. The lessons escalated. "Help yourself," said Mrs. D as she presented platters of dried grasshoppers, chocolate-covered bees and ants, and canned whale and bear. The degree to which we hesitated to chew a crunchy insect or longed for a grilled cheese sandwich while doing so was the degree to which we were bound to our culture, a somatic learning of "ethnocentric." With white chalk Mrs. D wrote the word on the blackboard. One class period she did the now-famous experiment designed by Jane Elliott: treat the blue-eyed students well and the brown-eyed students badly, then watch what happens.

In Sunshine City, we grew up fast. We were not seventh-graders but adults with our own lots in life. On our first day as residents in Sunshine City, we each drew a card from a bowl. The card assigned our name, age, race, occupation, and salary. The socio-economic demographics defined where we lived, and we moved to reassigned desks, our new neighborhoods. Susan drew her card, and it was a ticket to move to the right toward the wall; I drew mine and stayed on the left by the window, the track's wrong side.

Like most games, the goal of Sunshine City was to accrue points. Our individual point total determined our grade, which would carry significant weight for the quarter. In this honors class, we cared about grades. Points could be gained or lost in several ways. The way I remember it is that each identification card came with a predetermined, baseline set of points based on the given character's demographic characteristics. A white man came with more points than a white woman, who came with more points than a black man or a black woman. A doctor came with more points than did a mechanic.

Susan became a white businessman who owned the buildings in which lived most of Sunshine City's citizens who were seated with me on the left side of the room. I became a black man with a blue-collar job. From Susan's first card, she had enough points to get an A for the entire unit. When she moved to the right side of the room, she took a paperback book out of her bag and started reading. My card's baseline points suggested I was failing from the start, as were others in my neighborhood. A chorus of murmurs rustled from the room's left side, "unfair, unfair," as we calculated our grades.

A bowl of event cards circled daily, like a wheel on which people's lives continually turn, dealing each of us another round of weal or woe: laid off, lose 100 points; injured in car accident, lose 500 points; evicted from apartment, lose 200 points; promoted at work, gain 300 points; inherit money, gain 1,000 points. We could actively earn points by reading suggested books and writing book reports. Within the game's rules of play, we were free to do whatever we wanted for those two weeks.

Susan and I drew our daily cards from separate bowls, the contents of which were dictated by the algorithm set up by the initial card draw. Her cards were formalities and never budged her from setting the grade curve. While she alternated between reading mysteries and embroidering floral embellishment on a satin blouse, I read books from the reading list and wrote reports, during class time and also after school. Some days through a card draw, I lost whatever points I had earned by the report I just turned in. Once, Susan drew a card that raised my rent.

Those of us on the left side of the room voiced our righteous indignation. Surely Mrs. D would not grade us based on this game. Of course, we'd all played monopoly and clapped our hands to gain a house, traded up for hotels, and grabbed our money with each passing of Go, but this game taught hope and frustration beyond our years. Its outcome felt real and lasting. How do you work your way forward in a world when what you do and what is done to you all count the same on a score card?

"Of course you'll be graded," said Mrs. D with her proud and defiant curls. "Let your parents call."

Grown up and away from Sunshine City, in my neighborhood's morning sunshine, I walked back from the grocery store and bank and passed the homes of a preschool teacher, a daycare provider, a transportation specialist, more than one stay-at-home parent, an air traffic controller, a minister, a warehouse worker, a butcher, a baker, and a candlestick maker. Today and the next and the next, they open their doors and step outside. They back their cars out of driveways or hop on buses. The mail carrier walks among them sliding bills into mailboxes, relentlessly through snow and rain and heat. From the church tower, bells named for the four Gospel writers ring, marking the time.

~

With landing gear down and seats in their upright position, descent begins, my ears popping and stomach lifting. I enter the clouds where all is shrouded and hidden, hold my breath, and know that in the next moment or the next—when will it be?—all again will be sight. Coming up fast from below is the city and its towers and lakes. Finally, I breathe deep and open wide my eyes. There are the industrial parks and soccer fields, there the gridded streets. I look for the bell tower, the margin along the creek bed, the irregular shaped block, counting the driveways, the rooftops. There!

Along the fence at the back of my yard, one day many summers ago, a yellow daylily started blooming where there had been no bloom before. In secret, Bob had knelt on his grass, dug into his loamy soil, and lifted out the lily, dangly roots and all. He rose and crossed the yard line. In secret, he knelt again on our grass, dug into our soil, and laid those roots back down.

X marks the spot. How many cards have been drawn by now? Forward and back, by simple arithmetic the path unrolls. The points bought by work await calculation.

How efficiently Sunshine City delivered its lessons, lessons not just about racial and social inequity, but about definitions of success, rules of the game, inevitability of rank and status, and winds that blow tragic or comic. Of course the little game couldn't simulate life and work in its totality, but oh how the prospect of a single grade taught a single economy, as if there was only one path of forward progress to attend to and not the potential for one thousand and one side arcs inward and out, upward and back, each and every day, the trajectory of all together leading somewhere.

My eye is on the keyboard and the screen, the sky and the ground, in this interstice between space emptied and space waiting to be filled. My vision arcs from the taken to the given, between the seen and unseen, along the path of planes overhead. As Merton once asked, "How do you expect to arrive at the end of your own journey if you take the road to another man's city?"

The clock ticks, and I must finish the work. Its weight sits on my chest in a three-inch isosceles triangle, its peak hammered in at the jugular notch. At the upper eye socket, the cheek bones, the right shoulder, between the shoulder blades, behind the navel, and a hand's length above my knee, a cord stitches through and pulls tight.

TWO
Case Study

ON THE METHOD OF EXPLORATION

I t is morning, and from my landline I have dialed the call-in number for the conference call with a physician. The space between me and the people with whom I work spans miles, and our tools in common are computer and phone. The physician has a patient in mind. She knows him, has examined his body, taken his pulse, felt the rise of his chest under her stethoscope, palpated his abdomen.

Let's call the patient Mr. A.

The physician has shepherded Mr. A through the trials and tribulations of a disease and is on the phone to talk about it. The task at hand is to press this three-dimensional person and process across time onto the two-dimensional page. We are developing a case study. Mr. A may be unique in all human history, but as a patient for the purposes of this educational activity, he is a type. The goal here is that doctors who read his case study might better understand and care for any similar patient.

Mr. A is Everyman.

"What is our objective?" I ask at the start. We must have a destination in mind, an ending point that will shape the start and direct all that comes between. A final cause of sorts. The physician suggests two points, and I write those at the top of the notebook's blank page. I will refer to these points often, particularly when sorting among options for moving the case forward, like a breadcrumb trail laid in advance.

She begins to recite the facts. The 48-year-old man presented with intermittent stomach pain, heart palpitations, and fatigue of three-months duration. His physical examination was unremarkable. His personal medical history includes a ruptured Achilles tendon repaired two years prior and blood pressure in the range of stage I hypertension.

"What is Mr. A's job?" I ask when she pauses.

Her long breath sucked through the other end of the phone line followed by silence tells me this is an irrelevant question. I try again, "What does he do for a living?" More silence. I tell her facts like this help flesh out the patient into a person. Mr. A is not a stick figure, and I try to reconstitute the lost dimension in part with reminders of the human presence embodied in the text.

"Make him anything," she says.

Then a pause begins that I'm not sure I should interrupt. I wonder if she is asking me to supply this biographical piece as if indeed he could be anything. In that pause is all the tension between what you do not mattering and nothing mattering more than what you do. The coffee next to my notebook cools. The pause may never end.

On Monday mornings, my husband saves coffee for me in a thermos. He leaves about an hour before I get up for his group meeting. They don't call it a "job loss" group, but a "job transition" group, understandably wanting to put a positive spin on a negative situation. Four hundred men and women gather in a church sanctuary every Monday, spinning their hearts out. He wants his professional title back.

"Let's say Mr. A is a systems analyst," she finally says, and so we continue.

His family medical history includes diabetes in his mother and stroke in his paternal grandfather. What happens to parents sometimes has no small effect on their children, and pieces of the past must be filled in.

The patient's blood was inevitably drawn. The results? Chemistry panel and blood counts, normal.

~

I lift the notebook, turn the page over, and lay it back down, its metal spirals clicking against the desk surface. My cell phone vibrates and nearly shakes itself off the desk.

A case study is a teaching tool in which a patient's story is studied from many angles. Take a long hard look; poke around. In the classroom, this would take the form of a teacher-student dialog, but here on the written page, the learners confront multiple-choice questions, "Which of the following options...?" The questions usually focus on diagnosis, management, and prognosis. We operate on the honor system and list four answer options with the right answer identified immediately underneath. No peeking! I imagine the learners averting their eyes from the answer while deciding on a response.

Like Aquinas in his *Summa Theologica*, a discussion follows each question with an explanation as to why the right answer is right and the others are not. The rationale usually points to evidenced-based data, but sometimes when data are lacking or controversial, counsel based on the expert's experienced eye and trained mind prevails.

After each question-answer pairing, the patient's story picks up again, and he receives whatever the physician decided was best in terms of knowledge applied, test ordered, or treatment prescribed. Any discovery in terms of test result or patient response prompts the next question, and the cycle starts again until we come to the end.

The paper is white and cool under my hand, the pen solid between my fingers. The words flow fast and sloppy, abbreviated in a sort of shorthand that is not my usual penmanship. My thumb hurts from writing fast. The physician's job in this case study is to be the expert. My job is to ask questions and to write. Often I interrupt, "Please clarify." Or, "Say more about that." Or, "What is the reference for that number?"

Walter Canon first used the case study as a medical education tool in 1900, but Richard Cabot, a cardiologist, hematologist, clinical researcher, and Harvard Medical School educator, further developed it as a teaching tool, publishing *Case Teaching in Medicine: A Series of Graduated Exercises in the Differential Diagnosis, Prognosis and Treatment of Actual Cases of Disease* in 1907.

"The most important lesson to be learned by every student of medicine," Cabot wrote, "is the art of recognizing the physical signs of disease—a displaced cardiac apex, a succussion sound, an Argyle-Robertson pupil, a malarial parasite." He taught his students not only how to see but also how to join accurate and thorough physical data to a practiced reasoning process, writing, "After the student has learned to open his eyes and see, he must learn to shut them and think." What is the diagnosis? What is to be done? How will it end? The case study leads students to these final considerations.

Using this strategy, its only cost paper and time, students learned their lessons from true-to-life scenarios, the irrelevant and messy knotted together. "Then we can help the student to disentangle the essentials," Cabot wrote. They learned to reason well in spite of missing or hidden data. They learned the power of questions. Nothing was wasted, their past experience, learning, notes, and books, gathered together, mentally if not physically, in service to meaning.

The physician and I talk through all the questions, options, discussions, and patient events on the phone, but the final ordering happens after we hang up and I start writing. The pieces of the case study must tell a story by its end, a teleologically satisfying end given the beginning objective. A story can be told in multiple ways, but sometimes there is only one way in which it rings true and has a shape that pleases. Whereas the whole scope of the patient, what happened to him and what ails him, was amorphic but real, the case study as a written object requires giving a shape to the combined thought process and sequence of events.

Queries go back and forth between the physician and me in the days that follow as the writing of the case goes forward. I test her responses against published data; the National Library of Medicine is my friend. The goal is to accrue truth, to gather it from all corners.

I am at once worker, witness, and narrator, protagonist and minor character. I do the work; watch myself do the work; fill the page with and for the work of others; am the one on whom the work is working; and think about what it all means. More than one case study is in play. There is a condition to be explored, a discomfort to be evaluated, a longing to be quenched.

My personal work history includes: medical writer, laboratory consultant and educator; medical technologist in a genetics lab, general lab, and microbiology lab; lab assistant; teaching assistant; kitchen help; department store clerk; model; telephone solicitor; dinner theatre hostess; and babysitter. Wife and mother.

Virginia Woolf famously wrote, "Arrange whatever pieces come your way," and I find her advice nearly universally applicable. I play around with the pieces. Move them. Rename them. Order them based on what informs what. Order them within the bounds of rhetorical fair play. Order them with respect paid to time—and time is tricky; the effects of sequential events hold no allegiance to the clock or calendar and have no qualms about popping up in non-sequential order.

Sociologist Peter L. Berger calls the ordering gesture a "signal of transcendence." Gestures of play and hope are such signals too, he wrote, because they are all human behaviors or experiences that point to an ultimate reality that transcends the natural reality. In the case study, the ordering gesture is alive and well, ordering not just along timelines of cause and effect, and data and interpretation, but also along the continuum of illness to wellness, or at least not-quite-so-ill, with wholeness as the transcendent truth, beauty, and goodness that is the final prize.

Human literature is often scribbled in the margins. Margins of space. Of time. There, I flesh myself out with statements of occupation and questions of vocation. *What's really going on here?* I

write and doodle my way to an assessment of dreams and obses-
sions, fatigue and malaise, restlessness and straining. Prodromal
symptoms, work-related cause and effect, or simply red herrings?

My maternal grandfather fixed phone lines and preached. My
maternal grandmother colorized portraits with oil paints. My paternal grandfather was a farmer, took ill and lost his farm, then
sold Watkins products. My paternal grandmother served as her
town's postal clerk and worked as a secretary for the hardware
store on Main Street. My mother was a nurse. My father designed
flight control systems for rockets and spy planes, satellites, space
shuttles and space stations.

I'm calling on the strategies of Mr. Cabot, Ms. Woolf, Mr.
Aquinas, and Mr. Berger to explore the problem and what is to
be done. I aim to find the answers to the questions growing ever
larger in the margins; I aim for the longing for meaning to be met.
I aim to be satisfied.

As a child, I imagined what I would be when I grew up, what
work I would do. I played at working, and in my play I was a
teacher, nurse, mother, printer, dress designer, perfumer, librarian, writer, detective, and spy. I remember a favorite image: Leslie
Ann Warren in Rogers & Hammerstein's version of Cinderella
singing, "In my own little corner in my own little chair, I can
be whatever I want to be." It didn't occur to me then that to be
something was different than becoming, than living. When did I
start separating the two?

I open my eyes and see; shut them and think. I reorder and
rewrite. Disentangle the essentials from the messy knots of real
life; waste nothing; call on it all—experience, research, reflection,
expert opinion. I reorder the pieces again until they fit together

just right. This is how the case gets made; this is how the meaning emerges. Learners who read along can take with them clues and lessons to use in their own practice. The particular becomes universal.

Case studies rarely conclude with the patients all sewn up and good as new, but they usually walk taller and breathe easier. Once I read a paper in a medical journal that likened the patient to an airplane being readied for flight.

THREE
Summa Laborum I

ON WHAT IS GOOD WORK (A DEBATE)

> *Note: The three essays sharing the title "Summa Laborum," included here and in Acts II and III, are loosely based on the structure of debate in Thomas Aquinas's* Summa Theologica. *In* A Shorter Summa, *Peter Kreeft describes Aquinas's Summa as "a summarized debate. . .a shared journey of discovery." Each article in the* Summa *has five parts: first, a yes-or-no question; second, a list of responses that are in contrast to Aquinas's position, yet are nonetheless serious arguments regarding the posed question to be "considered and learned from"; third and fourth, combined in a single part here, his position, which usually points to an accepted written authority followed by an expansion of his position; and fifth, responses, paired to the first list, that show a different way of looking at the question.*

THE QUESTION

Should we expect work to be physically, mentally, and spiritually satisfying?

REASONS TO ANSWER YES

I. It seems that to sit back on an evening and call your work that day "good" is as fine a way to define satisfaction as there ever could be. In the Genesis record of creation, God did a day's or an eon's work and called it good. Another day, he did the same; and another; six times in total. He created, divided, brought forth, formed, and saw it all as good. He created man and woman—in the image of God, *imago Dei*, the record says—and declared them good. When considering the origin of the notion that work should be satisfying, we need go no further than this. There is no higher model.

2. When I think about my sons, I grieve even the thought of anything short of their satisfaction. Lord God, bless their nine-to-five days with ignited minds, bodies brimming with vitality, pride in accomplishment, joy and peace and gratitude. All this is my heart's desire.

3. Why not do what you like? It may be as simple and practical as that. When standing at the ice cream counter, why not choose chocolate truffle over maple nut if that is what will satisfy?

4. Work that meets certain standards—such as work that is for the good of society, or that stands the test of time, or that has your name stamped on it—presupposes satisfaction. Once these standards are met, satisfaction should result in the same way that two plus two equals four or blue mixed with yellow always makes green.

5. The experts say work should be satisfying. Dorothy L. Sayers, whose essay "Why Work?" prompted the posed question, argued that indeed work should bring physical, mental, and spiritual satisfaction. Frederick Buechner's guidance on the topic is often quoted with the same authority as Scripture, that "the place God calls you to is the place where your deep gladness and the world's deep hunger meet." Agrarians, artisans, and craftsmen write of the satisfaction that should arise from work as if it were the glow from rare wine sliding down their throats while dining at a private club.

∽

A Story

Once, long ago, I sat in a huddle with co-workers I'd only met that morning. From the huddle came an education. It was the first day of my first real job, the one that would pay my rent and launch me into the adult world of self-sufficiency. The position—medical technologist in a hospital microbiology laboratory—sprouted from a seed of passion, just like the literature of work says it should, and I had educated myself toward it.

The job had meaning, and it promised to satisfy. Learning clinical microbiology had been like discovering a parallel universe with its own encyclopedia of knowledge: the nomenclature, the growth requirements and biochemical distinctions, the mental algorithms, the physiology of the clinical infectious process. My senses were alive to it all: the agars poured in clear petri dishes—pale pink, celery green, mocha brown, blood red; the steel loop held solid in my hand and heated red in fire, my fingers guiding the loop's tip across the solidified agar surface; the constellation of colonies that emerged from nowhere after incubating overnight; the dyes that poured from glass bottles and stained organisms based on their proclivity to purple or pink, prelude to the moment of sliding the glass onto a microscope platform and pulling up a chair to see what I could see, eyes in position then focusing down to name the invisible; the lab itself, a chamber of musky and musty smells, stainless steel, and Bunsen burners. All that, plus I would be helping sick people get well.

Just after lunch on that first day, the six women who staffed the microbiology lab rolled their chairs and burden of labor over toward the microscopes to say they were mad as hell and weren't going to take it anymore. The time had come to vote, they said. The workload was too much to handle. Everyone was working late—without pay—in order to finish. After all, septicemia and surgical infections couldn't wait for the morning. The administration believed that if we could not finish the work by the end of each day shift, then the fault lay with us, not the system. Memo to staff who were paid by the hour and docked dollars and cents for minutes late: no pay for extra time and no one had better leave the premises with work still pending. Witness to the facts, I wrapped my white lab coat tight around my body, like a swaddled newborn.

History repeats itself. The story is ancient: today, make a quota of bricks from provided straw. Tomorrow, make the same quota from straw you collect yourselves. It is the stuff of strikes; of planned worker slow-downs; of high blood pressure and exhausted strength.

"Do we quit today, walk out now, all of us as one?"

The fiery supervisor was eager to lead the exit march. She and the manager had phases in which they didn't speak but passed notes through others. Every day, the manager made photocopies of any typos or errors of omission or commission detected in work notes and reports, no matter how minor. He held these copies in reserve should he ever want to fire someone on a moment's notice.

For reasons I no longer remember—but can guess were related to income and security—the women chose to bend to the burden awhile longer. They rose from their chairs and the huddle dispersed. I settled in and became one of them. Daily, we worked late without claiming the time on our timecards. We tried to think of new ways to respond to the accusation that the inability to absorb a malignant workload was our fault, but failed. Every afternoon, the manager walked to the copy machine, pieces of paper flapping in his hands, an insolent straight-ahead stare as he passed the lab's doorway. We took turns passing notes from supervisor to manager and back again.

There it is. There is the problem of work.

You take the first steps in a state of delight, equipped with skill or talent, ready to make a difference. But the path is never straight, and it takes you through places you never envisioned. Weeds and litter grow over the path.

Step around; step over.

You come away from any huddle with co-workers, any after-the-meeting meeting and remember the fall. Yes, Adam, the ground is hard. Yes, Eve, labor and feel the pain.

≈

Reasons to Answer No

1. I've just read about a new book that everyone's rushing to read, and I wonder if it is the one, the one at the end of a long line of attempts that finally shows the way to the joyful work we all can have. The one with a slogan or exhortation you tape to the mirror and review each morning. Or the set of bullets for which humankind has waited since receiving the curse—or prediction—just after the satisfied sigh of work called good: "Through pain and toil you will eat of [the ground] all the days of your life.... By the sweat of your brow you will eat your food." By this time in the story was God still satisfied?

2. I desire satisfaction for my sons at work and everywhere, but the examples that my husband and I have set, as well as our raising of them, suggest that they might expect otherwise from time to time. Sitting ringside at a match between job satisfaction and taking care of those you love and for whom you are responsible, the latter beats the former every time.

3. To satisfy is as small and simple as pleasing the senses and as large and complex as justifying one's life. The sensate choice that delivers the shot of satisfaction may not be what's on the table, and the larger eschatological conclusion is often reached in retrospect from a distant future.

4. No human arbiter has been appointed to judge whether one's link, well-intentioned but small, is or is not in the chain for society's good. The durability of work's outcome is but one plumb line of vocational meaning, and a timecard may be nonetheless precious despite having a number instead of a name. Even if we concede the high standards of utility, durability, and attribution, might not dissatisfaction yet visit the worker at an orphanage or at a potter's wheel or in a corner office with her name on the door?

5. I once watched a woman working behind a glass window at a popular restaurant. She removed a ball of dough from under a damp towel, rolled it with a rolling pin into the shape of a pancake, and set it on another damp towel. Over and over again, she rolled and rolled. Then she cooked each piece of rolled dough on a griddle, steam rising onto her chest and face, and stacked the finished tortillas. The customers were fed and happy, but her shoulders must surely ache. Teacher, poet, and priest Gerard Manley Hopkins, in a perpetual state of overwork, wrote, "My eyes are almost bleeding."

That arguments persist of satisfaction in the here and now as a universal measure of meaningful work—despite centuries of hard evidence about work's difficulty—is either the witness of non-universal experience, naïveté, or a courageous act of flying the flag of an unattainable ideal, like peace on earth, which we strive toward with hopes of improvement by increment. Even so, unattainable ideals attract our attention and respect, our efforts too. They suggest there may be something to find if sought. And so you commit your will to the search. In this case, the state of being satisfied is transformed from a passive judgment to the object of active effort—*I am* satisfied (or not) versus *I will be* satisfied.

FOUR
Metrics

ON MEASURING SIGNIFICANCE

1.

Contrary to the advertising you see in a magazine's glossy full-page spread in which the woman who has just taken a little blue, white, or pink pill smiles at the pill's success in resolving her insomnia, headache, or hypertension, not every individual who takes that pill is satisfied. Let's assume that competent and sincere researchers developed the pill in response to a human need; that an educated physician prescribed the pill in wholehearted concern for the patient's well-being, exactly according to its prescribing information approved by the United States Food and Drug Administration; that a dedicated pharmacist filled the prescription for the woman with accuracy and precision; that the woman, intent on being well, took the pill in full compliance with all dosing and administration directions. For this woman, this pill, although proven as an effective treatment, may or may not do for her what every player in this cascade of effort hopes.

2.

From a front window, I see the boy just after he has left my front door and now walks across the lawn to the neighbor's house. He can't be older than 14. A bulging white canvas bag hangs low on his thin frame and bounces off his shin with each step. I recognize this step, this bounce of the bag. Already he is reaching into the bag to take out the next paper. I know without looking that he has dropped a carefully rolled and rubber-banded free local newspaper on my front step. The paper is biweekly, but this is the first time I've witnessed its delivery and the deliverer. He is no longer anonymous. Did the boy notice the last copy of the paper he left, still bundled next to the flower planter? If so, this would not have been the first time. Brand me the revealer of a fact of life, a cause for disillusionment.

3.

The museum, with its limestone walls that have stood the test of time, houses fruits of labor granted registry on art and history's timeline. Glass, china, mahogany, canvas, fabric. Gold-leafed. Fired and blown, stained, painted, cut, woven. Here, now, alone in this glass case is not just a cup but rather a ceremonial drinking vessel AD 1681.

4.

In the cafeteria of a Florida hospital, where we ate biscuits and drank coffee and chocolate tea during morning breaks, a television was almost always on. The year was 1981, and we often saw coverage of the latest trials and tribulations of the Space Shuttle *Columbia* as the engineers and technical crew at NASA and the Kennedy Space Center, straight east across the state, worked for a successful first launch. My father was the engineering manager for the flight control systems. For years, long before "shuttle" was a household name or even a public curiosity, I knew what he was working on with his slide rule. He had first told us about it at the dinner table one night. The idea was wild. He rocked his hands in the air to show us the gyroscope action of the flight guidance instruments and then moved them along an upward then descending arc to show how the shuttle would launch like a rocket and land like a plane. He rested one hand on top of the other to show how it would return to the Center for its next launch by riding piggyback on a 747. After a disappointing launch pad test, a laboratory tech who spent her days with head bent down over a microscope rolled her eyes at the television. "Why don't they just give up?" she said. "That thing's never going to fly."

5.

It's raining hard, and the bag boy and I have six or so grocery bags in a cart. More than a quick dash away, my car is in the middle of the parking lot. In a flash, walking through the automatic door, the boy calculates potential outcomes. Off comes his rain slicker, and he tucks it over the groceries. When we reach the car, he and I both drip rain, but the cardboard cereal boxes, bag of flour, and Vidalia onions are dry.

6.

Students in Physics 101 learn that work is a transfer of energy. In equation form, work equals force times distance. Here's an experiment their teacher assigns: push a box across a table, and the force of pushing times the distance the box moved as a result of the pushing equals the amount of work done. They push and measure, jot their notes and calculations in a gridded lab notebook. What if the teacher had, in a concealed fashion, nailed the box to the table so that no matter how hard the box was pushed, it would never move? Or what if the teacher simultaneously pushed against the box from the other side? A student could push until he broke a heavy sweat, but the distance moved would be zero. Multiplying anything by zero equals zero. Despite the sweat, the student did no work. His energy failed to transfer to the object of his efforts. A body at work has no guarantees.

7.

A robin perches on top of my porch roof, overseeing things. Now on the rainspout adjacent to the evergreen arborvitae—from the Latin, "tree of life"—she hops from one square inch to another. The coast is clear, and she leaps into the tree. I think a nest hides within its branches, but I haven't wanted to investigate too closely for fear of scaring the brood. This tree has housed nests in the past but is too dense to see them from any distance. You must find a spot where the branches naturally part and move in close enough for the soft scale-like leaves to brush your cheeks. I cringe when a squirrel jumps into the tree and scurries up the trunk. One year, pale-blue robin eggs were on the ground, broken.

~

8.

Evidence-based medicine prizes a statistical concept called the "number needed to treat," or NNT. It describes a specific pharmacologic intervention's ability to achieve a stated outcome within a given population. The ability of a sleeping pill to produce a good night's sleep in a population of adults with insomnia, for example, or an analgesic's ability to relieve pain in people with a history of migraine headaches. With some interventions, the stated outcome could be the prevention of an adverse event. For example, the ability of a blood pressure medicine to prevent a heart attack or stroke in individuals with stage I hypertension. Derived from clinical trial data, the NNT tells how many people need to take a medicine in order for one person to experience the medicine's stated outcome. The NNT is seldom one. With the exception of antibiotics for certain kinds of infections, response rates to medicines are rarely 100 percent.

You can easily calculate the NNT given the right clinical trial data. First, find the percentage of people who experienced the intended outcome after taking the medicine, and subtract the percentage who experienced the same outcome after taking a placebo or control. Next, divide that number, in decimal form, into one. The sum of that equation is the NNT. For example, if 30 percent of people taking drug A have full relief from migraine headache within two hours and five percent of people taking a placebo have the same relief, then the $NNT = 1/[.30-.05] = 1/.25 = 4$. This means that four people need to take drug A in order for one of them to be headache-free two hours later due to the action of drug A.

~

9.

For one summer, my two sons—then 10 and 13 years old—delivered a weekly newspaper supplement that provided coupons and weekend entertainment tips. Each son had his own route. My older son did his route by himself, but I often helped the younger by driving papers to the end of strategic blocks or walking with him. Even if I walked with him, my son did the work. He rolled the papers with his brother earlier in the day or the night before, then loaded them into his white canvas bag and the car's trunk.

He carried the bag, bouncing against his shin with each step, and placed the papers carefully next to each door; no wild pitches. Whenever we came to a certain house on a corner lot, I wanted to divert his attention to the other side of the street and place the paper on the stoop myself. I wanted to shield his eyes, as parents do, when a child is about to encounter a fact of life too soon. My son saw but seemed not to care. He'd lay the paper down on top of the other papers—some now yellowed, many wet and soggy—that he had carefully rolled and delivered weeks and weeks before, an ever-growing mound. His work at this house seemingly wasted. Sometimes he'd shrug his shoulders as if to say, "What's wrong with them? Their loss." His eye was on finishing his route and collecting his pay. An evidence-based assessment would have concluded that delivery at this house was not worthwhile, but my son had signed his name that every address would get a paper—and his boss had told him, "I do spot checks sometimes." His boss, however, could not require him to ensure that every recipient read or even open the paper, let alone clip the coupons or patronize the advertised events.

10.

There, under the chairs now askew at the banquet tables come meeting's end: papers and booklets left creased and dirty to be gathered by janitors and tossed. Let me calculate the hours of work per abandoned page. The projector off and cooling, the PowerPoint slides—edited, fact-checked, bulleted, graphed, colored, formatted—go dark. Online, documents I researched and crafted have been transferred to digital code and uploaded, only to be deleted at some future time like a light turned off. Get them before they're gone! "I throw away everything you send me," a customer once told me on a job long ago.

11.

Two taps on a rock for water in a desert-long obedience, and Moses loses entrance to the Promised Land. Still the water gushed, and hundreds of thousands of thirsty people drank. Heidegger taught perspectival thinking: "Calculative thought places itself under compulsion to master everything in the logical terms of its procedure.... Essential thinking looks for the slow signs of the incalculable and sees in this the unforeseeable coming of the ineluctable."

12.

Take the total cost in money or hours and divide by the number of people served. Multiply by the immediate profit. Multiply again by the guess at future business generated. Divide by the square root of possible benefit to be appreciated at an undiscoverable rate over time without end to all parties fanning out to the nth degree into perpetuity. Multiply by the derivative of unknown harm averted—or done—to the same population. The calculus of value thwarts calculation.

13.

An offering laid out on a rock may or may not be set ablaze. The spark, energy transferred from some divine tip like the transcendent flash from writer to reader, the mark of the sublime as per Longinus. Dare I use the term *sublime* to cover a day's work? In two syllables, overwhelming force meets awe. A prophecy of sorts, a blessing, an aesthetic to shape what comes to pass.

14.

The tram at the Minnesota Landscape Arboretum rocked and swayed along the property's three-mile drive. To your right, said the tram's driver and tour guide, to your left. No need for us riders to figure out where to look or what we're looking at. Just listen and look. Breathe the air spiced with azalea, lilacs, and pines—Colorado, Pondorosa, white, and red; someone planted them all years ago. Just beyond those red maples, wild flowers wait beside paths. Lots of lady's slippers now, said our guide. I planned to see my first.

We passed a research area where plant breeders were in the third season of testing rhododendron cultivars. (All azaleas are rhododendrons, but not all rhododendrons are azaleas, she told us as an added bonus fact.) Which can best survive our winters? Which can grow in our soil, so clay-like and alkaline? First, the breeders had to work on the soil, she said, to increase drainage and acidity. It took a whole summer just to accomplish that. Then came the winter test: which strain would still be standing—and flowering—come the next spring? And which could last yet one more winter? Last forever? So slow the progress. Digging, planting, feeding, pruning, measuring, watering.

FIVE
First Author, et Al., ad Infinitum

ON WHO GETS CREDIT

> My hand made an instrument, and my fingers fashioned
> a psaltery.
> And who shall tell my Lord? The Lord Himself, He
> Himself shall hearken.
>
> —A Psalm of David

My husband's father was a lifelong engineer at the company that introduced the first transparent adhesive tape and sticky notes. When he died, we buried him in the shadow of a cedar and two blue spruces on a hill overlooking a lake in Minneapolis. The spot is marked with a flat gravestone, granite no wider or taller than a breadboard, engraved with his name and the years of his birth and death. Inserted into the foot end of his poplar wood casket is a tiny glass vial containing a paper with his full name. The funeral director explained, "In case there's ever any question." To the east, not more than 15 feet, stands a granite marker, large as a city gate, displaying the name of a man who had been a Minnesota state representative, a name you can find on a map.

Think: Father Hennepin and Saint Paul, Humphrey, Guthrie, Lindbergh, and Brothers Mayo with their respective namesakes—county and capital, institute, theater, airport, and clinic.

A photograph of Lady Bird Johnson, taken by Frank Wolfe in 1990 and housed in the Lyndon Baines Johnson Presidential Library charms me. Wearing a turquoise sweater and a red-banded straw hat, she is sitting in a field of Texas wildflowers, red and yellow Indian Blankets. This picture circulated widely in the media after her death in 2007 at the age of 94. The evening news flashed it across the screen. The broadcaster would not even have had to say her name for the audience to know whom the story was about. Her work in conservation and beautification needed no description, particularly with native plants, because the flowers symbolized her work. Lady Bird's identity and her work facilitating wildflowers were so well known that the questions commonly posed at dinner parties—"Who are you? What do you do?"—were unnecessary. Cecil Stoughton took a more famous picture of Lady Bird on November 22, 1963, aboard Air Force One, but in that picture, Stoughton draws his viewers' eyes first not to Lady Bird but to the woman on the right, who at that very moment was becoming the former First Lady, and to Lady Bird's husband, his right hand raised.

Think: Einstein and relativity, the Wright Brothers and the airplane, Leeuwenhoek and microscopes.

"What is the reference?" I ask, ever in search of a primary source. The question comes when the findings of a study are offered up as a clinical rationale, when a bar graph is entered as evidence, or when data are put into use for a medical writing project. I ask it of the supplying party or of myself, and a search begins. Data must be linked to a study, and the study must be published in a paper or presented in an abstract or poster at a medical meeting. Its first author, literally the name that appears first on the document's byline, forever identifies that document.

> [Insert First Author name] published that data.
> Didn't [insert First Author name] present that abstract?

I've witnessed researchers at meetings, seated at conference tables placed at perpendicular angles to achieve the perfect square to ease hierarchical strain; their laptop computers open in front of them; bottles of artesian water and bowls of hard candies waiting beyond the crystal drinking glasses; microphones placed at even intervals, wired and tested to pick up every percent and decimal point. They toss around data so easily, so quickly, like primal words of a mother tongue. But I have to interrupt: "Where is it written?" Baseline demographics, percent responses, P-values, hazard ratios, and relative risks come from somewhere, and this question is how you find out where. Answering this question is how you confirm that numbers were not transposed; that decimal points were not dropped; that conclusions drawn can be substantiated in black and white.

The project now on my desktop has 39 cited papers. I've inserted the respective 39 first author names into brackets within the electronic manuscript so many times that I could list those names with my eyes closed. Yet, I know not one of the other 159 names on those 39 papers, the authors listed second and beyond.

> That's the [insert First Author name] paper isn't it?
> Get me that paper by [insert First Author name].

The tenth edition of the *American Medical Association Manual of Style* states that a paper's first author position should go to the one who did the most work, with other authors listed in order of degree of contribution. The manual also states, "Disagreement about order should be resolved by the authors, not the editor." Journal style guides differ slightly regarding how a paper is cited in a bibliography, but generally any names after the first three or four are subsumed under et al., and common oral usage subsumes all but the first.

Think: Karl Landsteiner and human blood groups, Rueben Ottenberg and cross-matched blood transfusion, Jonas Salk and the polio vaccine, Max Perutz and hemoglobin's structure, Christiaan Barnard and heart transplant.

I do my work partly by searching for the work of others in MED-LINE®, the National Library of Medicine's online database. At the time of this writing, the database archives more than 21 million citations from more than 5,600 biomedical journals. Such a volume of accumulated documents is approximately equivalent to what would be produced if everyone in New York City proper and Moscow combined wrote a paper of his or her lifetime discoveries, and an unseen someone indexed and entered them into perpetuity.

Once, our family vacationed in Washington, DC, visiting monuments, memorials, buildings, and streets named for the likes of Washington, Lincoln, Kennedy, Hoover, Penn, and Smithson. We visited the Vietnam Veterans Memorial, now listing 58,272 names. We waved to the President riding in his black limousine. I insisted on a side trip to Bethesda to visit the medical library in true versus virtual reality, as if it were a pilgrimage.

I expected something grander (think: Library of Congress) than its nondescript brown exterior on a slight rise of land, lawn cut short under the hot summer sun. I took pictures while my sons rolled their eyes. Inside, I saw the reading room and looked into the offices of men and women whose work makes my work possible. They add 2,000 to 4,000 new citations per day to the library's database nearly every week, Tuesday through Saturday.

Think: custodians and computer programmers of the whiz kid's laboratory; the technicians who sterilize equipment for successful bone grafts; the typists of seminal papers; the botanists and gardeners whose work is absorbed into the lifting and swaying fringed landscape; the women working in church basements and the men in their prayer closets; the et al., ad infinitum who daily propel forward currents of excellence and beauty and integrity, no matter the current's first cause.

A tag sewn on the inside lining of a favorite summer handbag bears a name printed in indelible ink: "Romana Z~", the R like a scissors, the Z like a rippled thread. Romana, a woman I've never met, sewed this backpack-type handbag of green and gold wheat-print cotton with an indigo denim cord that I bought on the sidewalk at Bleecker and Carmine in Greenwich Village on a sunny September day. Wendy Luker sold me the bag. She and I talked for a while as I fingered fabrics and tested shoulder straps. She told me she started Wendyloo Handbags as a recovery effort after the strain of graduate school. She intentionally gives honor and dignity to the women who work for her as seamstresses by having each one sign the bags she sews. Thus, Romana's name signed on my bag.

By digging, you can usually—but not always—find my name on the projects for which I'm hired. Usually it's a footnote, the unseen, unspoken end of the credits. I often watch films to the end as the final footage lists the plenum of contributing names, absorbing the last moments of the theater atmosphere, listening to the soundtrack's finale, but admittedly I stop reading the names soon after those of the cast roll by. The hairstyle assistants, prop managers, and dog trainers go without a witness. Sometimes my name can't be found on a project no matter how hard you dig, if even you cared to.

There is plenty of debate about names: who leaves their mark and where they leave it. Once, the top-billed author of a project I worked on raised an objection to the footnote that attributed the writing of the piece to me, as if the footnote implied the content was my intellectual property rather than his. The objection required me to justify my role to him and my life to myself.

I read the words of the psalmist, "My heart is not proud." If I claimed the same for myself, the cumulative time I spend questioning myself about being only the conduit for others' expertise would testify against me—not First Author, not Original Thinker, not Maker of a Whole, neither Mover nor Shaker.

Think: false god. Fiercely tempting, erected by well-meaning motivational speakers and experts, but a god as absurd as the golden calf that stood inert, unaware of how many contributed earrings, bracelets, and charms melted into its making. Even Lady Bird didn't plant all the flowers she sat among.

I've watched a First Author enter a team project meeting and shake hands with only those persons of matching credentials, walking past the rest with his eyes tracking ahead and his hand reaching over our heads. Minutes later, I watched another First Author—credentials weightier than any in the room—enter and shake hands with every person: audio-visual technicians, medical writer, and all. The author looked at each eye-to-eye. I've forgotten the face of the first; I'll always remember the face of the second.

At the store where I buy printer paper, I wonder about a former cashier's story. She used to walk that neighborhood's business district mumbling to herself, with mismatched, dated clothes and uncombed hair. The coffee shop would give her small glasses of water and free sample-sized cups of coffee, which she would carry back out the door and sip as she walked.

Then one day, she stood behind the cash register, neatly dressed, helping customers. When I first saw her there, I breathed a sigh of relief for her and the sweeping newness in her life. I wondered about the story that gave her a job and about how her life changed when her name appeared on a work schedule and a plastic name tag. But then she was gone.

I miss buying paper from her. We pass sometimes on a sidewalk or at an intersection in that neighborhood and I want to tell her this, but something stops me. Fear that she would reject my words. Concern that she may not want to be seen or that being seen would trigger a grief. Recognition that in a burst of personal agency she may have happily shaken a minimum wage job's dust off her feet. Shame that I had delighted over her name tag yet don't remember her name.

SIX
Breath and Blood

ON GIVING YOUR LIFE

> My respiration and inspiration, the beating of my heart,
> the passing of blood and air through my lungs....
>
> —Walt Whitman, *Song of Myself*

The average adult takes 17,000 or more breaths per day, but my guess is that a man or woman seated at a computer for eight of the 24 hours takes considerably fewer. The screen steals your breath. With eyes locked on the rectangular monitor, forearms raised and hands on the keyboard, my back against the chair, I forget to breathe. Thirty or more breathless seconds go by as if underwater. Oxygen drops and carbon dioxide rises, triggering a series of physiologic responses that ultimately increase my blood pressure. When I break the surface, the inhalations pull shallow and insufficient. This cycle repeated enough times, I stand, throw back my shoulders, expand my belly, shake limbs, gulp air.

The document on my computer and the papers around my desk are about blood gone wrong. It is about hemoglobin misshapen. Go to a doctor, and you'll likely get a finger pricked and your red blood cell hemoglobin measured in grams per deciliter. In hemoglobin, breath and blood meet.

The hemoglobin molecule is a tetramer, consisting of four globin chains, two alpha and two beta, wrapped around a heme unit that holds iron at its center. In the lungs, hemoglobin grabs freshly inhaled oxygen by binding one molecule to each heme unit. As oxygenated blood moves through the body, hemoglobin releases oxygen into the tissues as needed, like a paper carrier who drops a paper at each doorstep.

A mutation on the short arm of chromosome 11, a substitution of glutamic acid for valine in one or both of the beta globin chains, is all it takes to be born with a variant hemoglobin molecule. Hemoglobin S is the culprit responsible for sickle cell disease. A red blood cell with normal hemoglobin, hemoglobin A, moves through its route—from lungs, through the body, and back again—never losing its flexible concave shape even when passing through tight spaces, like a disk of set gelatin you can push and watch spring back. Hemoglobin S, in contrast, turns rigid when oxygen is lacking, causing the red blood cells to take the shape of a sickle, particularly in people with a double-dose mutation.

I've seen sickled cells under a microscope, stiff and crackled. These cells don't last long in circulation, about 17 days for a cell with two hemoglobin S molecules compared with 120 for cells with normal hemoglobin. Their shape prohibits easy movement through small blood vessels, causing blood flow obstruction, pain, tissue and organ damage, infections, anemia, stroke, and early death. This current project, my piece and the whole program of which it is part, takes aim at the morbidity and mortality associated with this disease.

You can buy an electronic gizmo that claims to give back the breath computers steal. Downloaded and installed on a computer's desktop, an image that resembles a balloon expands and shrinks like lungs in the process of normal breathing. The program's operating premise is that you'll see the mock respirations out of the corner of your eye and imitate with the real thing. Between commas you restore your life, keep it going to the next period when it will be time again to inhale, exhale. Breathe. Live.

The air smells of rubbing alcohol. I have left the sickle cell document open on the computer, and in response to a call, stepped away from my office for a couple hours. Just inside the doorway, to my left, a young woman sits in front of a computer screen. Further to my left, beyond the desk, is a counter with cupboards above and a dorm-sized refrigerator below. I know, from previous visits, that the refrigerator holds small plastic bottles of juice, bottled water, and soft drinks. To the right, against the window, is a round table covered with magazines and newspapers. On a counter behind the table is a coffee maker and a large, clear, plastic cookie bin. The walls are white with crooked papers taped at infrequent intervals.

Welcome to the blood bank.

Stomach, tense; throat, tight. I'm a child again, in a doctor's office, waiting for a shot. I'm a student again, in a hospital blood bank, learning to slide large bore needles into the vein of the antecubital fossa, learning to type and cross-match blood for transfusions by pipetting drops of red blood cells and plasma into test tubes. Centrifuge and look for clumps. Mistakes are deadly.

The woman at the desk says hello and asks for my driver's license. She hands me a laminated paper that lists the places I should not have traveled and things I should not have done if I want to donate blood.

"We have an urgent need for your blood type," the caller on the telephone had said. The need is never less than urgent because this, or some variation, is what they always say when they call. Until recently, I'd gone a couple years ignoring the blood bank's phone calls. When the world started collapsing into financial ruin, however, in a burst of citizenry I started picking up the phone.

"I'm ready for you." The phlebotomist is wearing a white pant-suit uniform and a white lab coat. "Laurie," she says, flashing me the badge clipped to her coat. She leads me into a closet-sized room and closes the door behind us. In the room are two chairs, a desk, a computer, a shelf of papers and books, and a bulletin board. On a corner of the desk is a red medical instrument the size of a pocket camera. We both sit, she in front of her comput-er. "Your full legal name?" I tell her. She types, pauses, and looks at her screen. She turns away from the computer and reaches for my hand, wipes the left middle finger with rubbing alcohol, then pricks it with a lancet. She milks my finger from its base to the tip until a pearl-sized drop of blood forms. She dips a clear plastic cuvette into the blood to draw it in, then places the cuvette in the instrument. "15.4," she says. "You're healthy as a horse."

Next, Laurie places a thermometer under my tongue, and while I hold it there, she presses her pointer and middle finger on my wrist in the space between the tendons, where the radial artery pulses below the surface. Neither of us talks while she looks at her watch and counts: beat, pause, beat, pause, beat, pause, beat. The heart pumps blood into expanding and contracting blood vessels, creating a palpable tap from below as if something alive is buried and wants you to know it's there. Concealed vitality, revealed. Western medicine finds and takes one pulse. One number—say 65—that tells how fast your heart is beating, which in turn suggests a state of health or lack thereof. The beat, a flutter or a throb. The pause, sometimes longer, sometimes shorter. Everything is ever and always more than what it seems.

Far from the clear, literal instruction of press and count, Chinese medicine takes no pulse but palpates 12 openings, six on each wrist, reading the state of health of multiple organs, not only that of the heart. Medical historian Shigehisa Kuriyama writes that practitioners of Chinese medicine feel for something other than blood, some other vital force I don't understand. They feel for *mo*. Each day, *mo* makes about 50 circuits of the body, one circuit for every 300 or so breaths.

Out of a drawer, Laurie pulls a blood pressure cuff. I roll up my sleeve. Wrap; pump, pump, pump, pump; slow release. She listens through the stethoscope at her ears to the sounds of systole and diastole transmitted by the silver-topped diaphragm she has placed on the underside of my elbow. She types more, stands, and motions for me to take her seat at the computer. Eyes to screen, here is where the remaining vital sign—respiration—could fail me, but she doesn't check. "You've done these questions before, just open the door when you're done," she says.

The voice on the computer welcomes and instructs me, then the questions begin. Have you ever...? Have you ever...? With each donation, the list gets longer. Years ago, before this interview was computerized, phlebotomists asked screening questions face-to-face, trying hard to be casual and keep their eyes on the paper as they asked things like, "Have you ever traded sex for money or drugs?" or "Have you ever had sex with a man who had sex with a man?" Today, my list of no's satisfies the computer's internal algorithm, but there are questions that go unasked: *Have you anything inside to spare? What is the cost for giving what you have?*

Laurie escorts me to the drawing room. No bigger than a large bedroom, it houses two brown vinyl drawing chairs that look like recliners, a counter with a sink, cupboards, and a refrigerator. I take a seat. Laurie straightens out my right arm; ties rubber tubing tight about three inches above the elbow; palpates the blue vein at the elbow's crease, turgid now from the tourniquet's pressure; marks its course with a black marker; unties the tubing; swabs the region with Betadine until the skin is yellow-brown. "Squeeze this," she says and places a white plastic cylinder inside my fist. She reties the tubing and unsheathes her needle. The slippery vein threatens to pop out of place so she anchors it above and below with her index finger and thumb. I hold my breath. There's the sting. In slides the needle.

The physical takes over without effort. My blood flows into the tubing and then into the blood unit bag, both made of plastic the color of rice water. The goal is 500 cc. Laurie tapes the needle in position and then places the bag on a machine that gently tips it forward, then back, forward, then back, allowing the blood and the bag's liquid anticoagulant to mix. Ch-chee, ch-chee, ch-chee. The bag slowly fills with blood that my bone marrow made weeks or months ago.

Get a soup bone, and touch the spongy marrow. If it were living tissue in a breathing body, red blood cells would be popping out like babies from a preemie nursery: mature, move on, and do what you were made to do. At the end of a cell's lifespan, the body recycles the globin chains and iron, operating as it does with a nothing-important-is-wasted *modus operandi*.

I squeeze the cylinder every few seconds to keep the blood flowing fast. While the bag fills, Laurie and I talk. She tells me that her husband has been laid off. He can only give his work away free to friends while he waits for another union job. She sighs, smiles, and offers me a choice of pink, blue, purple, or green bandaging.

She gives me a four-color, glossy brochure to take home, a kind of thank you. The cover shows a young boy who is alive somewhere in three dimensions because of donated blood.

"You helped save a life like Trey's today," the brochure says. The text continues on to say that within minutes of transfusion, Trey is running and playing as if he never had sickle cell disease.

I don't spill blood for my work; I don't even break a sweat. I write and take my diminished breaths. Expand, contract, expand, contract, expand, contract. I sit and think and write and my work gets done. Beat, pause, beat. Here is a sentence about transfusion requirements; here is a paragraph about complications. I wonder about the physicality of the blood in the bag versus the electronic document on my computer screen, both in service to the same disease. Inside me, 3 million red blood cells expire for each second the document grows. *Have you anything to fill you back up?*

Laurie told me to drink some juice and eat a cookie before I left, to sit down at the table and take as much time as I needed. She told me to not skip a meal that day and to not lift anything heavy. Take it easy. Let your body get used to less blood while the marrow replaces what was donated. "You may feel tired," she warned. I drank a bottle of cranberry juice then ate a chocolate chip cookie and a box of raisins. I took a bottle of water for the trip back to my office. In the span of that 15-minute drive, the blood cells that remained coursed through my body 45 times. In 56 days, I can give again.

Like a swollen river overflowing its banks, the project gushes beyond its time and scope projections. My phone rings, and it's an unexpected conference call, "Hi, you're on speakerphone." Another scheduled project begins on top of it. I work Saturdays, and on Sundays wake up feeling drugged. For weeks after donating, taking a walk does me in. In the afternoons, I fight the urge to nap; dinners don't get made. This is more than what I lost through the needle. Perhaps I had less to spare than we figured.

My first babysitting job came at about the age of 12. I started to calculate the worth of something that cost money by its equivalent in time spent watching the neighbor's children. Years later, in high school, I worked at part-time jobs and continued the calculations. Is it worth working X hours to buy Y? Is Z worth a weekend shift? It's been a long time since I've multiplied and divided in such a way. New calculations now suggest themselves.

Journal articles printed on white paper are sorted in piles on the floor around my chair, my handwritten notes in their margins. Hard copy versions of the manuscript in progress are stacked beside them. On the computer, the list of electronic versions stretches to fill a long column. In the spaces between the notes, the words, the lines, and the pages, between the getting up and the sitting back down, breathe in, breathe out. Let the meaning mix and percolate down. In this body of work, only at the end can I see if the whole hangs together.

Each eight-hour workday that I choose to sit at this desk means I also choose that here is where 86 billion red blood cells will be spent. How many breaths, how many circuits of vital force does a day cost? The blood that was in my body at the project's start is long gone by its finish five months later. I've taken no oath to give my blood for this cause that is my job, but what else are we doing every day if not giving our lifeblood for the task at hand?

I start to use a virtual bell on the computer to remind me to breathe. Every 15 minutes the bell's clapper strikes its lip and the sound pulls me from the deep like a saving hand. Oxygen and peace kiss. Three long full breaths from the belly, and the slow sink begins again.

On a medical writing Listserve to which I belong, a woman asks, "Does anybody know whether I can insert a thin space in Word?" I save this email and wait for the responses that come, but no one else reads the question and its unintended double meaning with the same longing for a *thin space,* meaning a flutter, a throb, of deep reality, to open within a day of work.

"What's that?" my client asks when she hears the bell in the background as we talk on the phone. I try to think of a funny response, but only the truth comes, and so I say, "It reminds me to breathe." She laughs as if I had told a joke she doesn't understand.

ACT II

Where we encounter rest and contemplation; time and space; beauty, prayer, and faith; imagination; an urge for freedom; a dual job description; people and moments worthy of pause; bills that keep coming and a pink slip.

Six days a week the spirit is alone, disregarded, forsaken, forgotten. Working under strain, beset with worries, enmeshed in anxieties, man has no mind for ethereal beauty. But the spirit is waiting for man to join it.

—Abraham Joshua Heschel, *The Sabbath*

SEVEN
Still in French Airspace

ON LOOKING OUT AND UP

I am not an easy flyer. I'm afraid of falling from the sky. Before nearly every flight, a ring of olive wood prayer beads encircles my right middle finger, its dangling cross presses against my palm's flesh. The preflight donning of this ring is a habit born not of religious fervor but of fear. Where the boundary is between talisman and reminder of faith I'm not sure. As the engines roar and the plane begins the rush down its sapphire- and ruby-studded runway, "God of grace and mercy" begins its repetitions in my mind like a preprogrammed tape.

A pilot friend claims that planes are built to fly. I try to remind myself of this when unseen turbulence rocks and jiggles a plane on which I travel. Despite all appearances to the contrary, turbulence portends no cause for alarm because the plane and the space through which it flies are in harmony. The plane's design and materials are suited to its state of being with 30-some thousand feet of space below it and an immeasurable amount of space to the sides and above. The space accepts the entry of fiberglass, aluminum and steel, fabric and Plexiglas, the in-transit women and men.

Sometimes pilots announce expected turbulence over the public address system, and when they do I am always grateful for the advance explanation for the rough ride ahead, but they seldom say anything during the course of an uneventful flight that makes you grab a pen, write down the words, and remember them forever. On the first leg of a flight home from an overseas work project the pilot did in fact say something memorable, a six-word interruption to the murmur, pop, and swish of flight attendants opening, pouring, and passing one soft drink after another across the laps of passengers that made me perk up and take note: here was a clue. Let him with ears hear and I had heard.

"We are still in French airspace," the pilot said.

Maybe all that was needed to pique this Midwesterner's attention was the mere mention of anything "French," maybe it was jet lag's fatigue, maybe it was the droning hum of the plane's engines lulling me into a state of near hypnotic suggestibility. I took my notebook out of my bag and wrote down the pilot's words. I wondered what else could come of his statement and felt sure something would.

This was not the geographic remark that pilots routinely make: "If you look out the right side of the plane you'll see the lights of Cincinnati," or "We'll be flying over Lake Michigan just ahead." Instead, *"We are still in French airspace"* hinted a grander intention, pointing not to a single geographic site below that would be gone in a flash but highlighting a state of being, a view of parallel reality.

The pilot offered more for my imagination to unwrap than his words at face value, like an Old Testament prophet whose poetry telescoped layer upon layer of meaning across a timeline to when men and women will dream dreams and beyond. Vines and figs, stars and sun are never just what they seem, and references to boundary lines mean far more than territorial rights.

We are still in French airspace. Why had the pilot said these words for his passengers? He may have watched us board and seen some whose holiday had not been long enough, or worse, had never begun. What gave us away? Perhaps it was the barely used travel guides peeking out from pockets of carry-on luggage or the last-minute souvenirs bought in airport shops and cradled in our arms as we made our way down the aisle to our seats. Maybe it was the remnant of longing in our gaze.

At the age of 23, poet Rainer Maria Rilke wrote *Stories of God,* a book of 13 connected stories that an unidentified narrator tells to his neighbors and assorted nonhuman listeners, such as the clouds and the dark. Pass the stories along to the children, he said.

In the book's first story God creates man, although the story may be more accurately summarized by saying that after God shaped man's face from clay, he let his hands finish the task while he instead turned his eyes toward earth. God wanted to see what was happening with what he had already created; time racing below as it did, he didn't want to miss a thing. God gave strict instructions to the hands: show me the final product before sending the man down to live. He wanted to see what a human was like.

A terrible accident happened while God waited for the great unveiling. The finished man fell from the heavens to earth. Whether the hands dropped him or the man propelled himself—"in such a hurry to live"—was a matter of dispute. By the time the confusion settled and God looked down through space, an instant had passed, a thousand years had passed, and already a million men and women populated the earth, clothed in a fashion that "distorted people's faces badly."

God couldn't get a good look and so his question remained, What is a human like? The narrator says there are those who yet try to answer.

Planes flying from Barcelona to Amsterdam take off from Aeroport del Prat, pausing as planes do at the runway's start before the rush of takeoff and ascent. They skim the dark turquoise water of the Mediterranean, then turn and rise up over the Pyrenees. At cruising altitude, when the ride is smooth, passengers relax and flight attendants push their beverage carts down the aisle. Seated at a window in row eight or thereabouts, I drank tea with milk and sugar served in a china cup with saucer.

We are still in French airspace.

Buckled in tight and with the pilot's approval, I was not yet back at my desk. I was still someplace else, traveling, on an adventure. I could stop replaying the past days' conversations and pitfalls; ignore the workload stowed in the briefcase under the seat; forget the projects waiting for me on the desk back home. The pilot pointed to a spacious place. Barcelona may have been lost, but we still had France.

Outside, the cloudless sky hugged the plane, its brilliant blue pressing against the white of the wings and fuselage. The French countryside spread far into the horizon. I imagined we were passing over a French village, with its *fromagier* and *patisserie.* The plane's shadow grazed the path of a woman who walked from the market, a baguette peeking from her cloth shopping bag, then skimmed the table where a man sat in the sun raising a glass of merlot.

From the space of my basement office, I had worked for two months on part one of this project for a client who then sent me an ocean away to help execute the project's part two, exchanging one basement office for another. In part one, version after version of Word and PowerPoint files moved back and forth between my desktop and that of my client and the physicians who were the project's faculty. Work, rush, work. At night, I had lain awake while my computer slept and mentally subtracted household and college expenses from what had once been two incomes but now was one, aiming for a sum that was black. In the project's part two, the same group of players sat around a rectangular table in a Barcelona hotel's basement conference room of white walls, blue carpet, and blue drapes that only covered the absence of windows. Work, rush, work.

I often dream dreams about work. Here's one: *A man, a composite of several past bosses, lays out contracts for new work. He offers me a pen and asks me to sign the papers. Instead I slip away. At the last minute I run to find him, but when I do, the pen is there but the contracts are gone. Did I sign them or didn't I? My dream character isn't sure. I fear that I did not and have lost the opportunity for work; I fear that I did and have lost my freedom.*

And another: *A different boss composite brings out a calendar and asks for volunteers to sign up for shifts drawing blood, a laboratory-oriented task I haven't done in decades, never liked nor was particularly good at. I write my name in all the time slots, and as I do, I know that I am forfeiting my work for hers.*

And another: *Two men with whom I used to work see me enter a crowded room. "There you are," they shout. Before I can escape, they pull me over to a table and proceed to engage me in a job that I left years ago. I scream.*

Sometimes, if you're not careful, livelihood crashes. Livelihood as in the way of one's life and the provision—material and immaterial—to make that way possible. And isn't that the crux of it? To make your way in the world in every sense of the word, to keep it all flying forward.

How had the pilot known that he was captain for the weary and heavy laden? Could he smell the fear? Fear of need exceeding provision, fear of responsibility exceeding capability, fear of losing ourselves in a free fall through clouds of must-dos and to-dos and can't-do-it-anymores. The belts in our claustrophobic seats choked; could we find a lighter yoke?

When you look at the face of a worker, wrote Josef Pieper, what you see is effort and stress becoming permanently etched. I've been reading and re-reading Pieper's *Leisure: The Basis of Culture* for a book group called "Sophia," because, like the Greeks, this group seeks wisdom. I think it's true what is said, that when the student is ready, the teacher appears. It's also true that when you set your mind on a search, posit a question, you start seeing clues.

Years before, someone whose opinion I respect recommended the book, and in a spirit of dutiful response, I checked it out of my local library. The book was small with a worn gold hardcover, no dust jacket, and yellowed pages. Copyright 1952. I had flipped from page to page, dipping here and there into the dense writing. I'll skip it, I thought. To read this book would take too much time in a schedule filled with too much work. I already knew what it said, didn't I? That it was in periods of leisure, among people who could afford leisure, that the extras that pushed society forward arose. The discoveries of geometry and calculus came about from men with time on their hands, not from men laboring deep down in a mine. The exquisite textiles that now hang in museums were woven by hands not otherwise occupied stirring gruel. I knew these pieces of history. It wasn't hard to extrapolate the principle to the present. The book was as good as read without completing a single full paragraph. I returned the book to the library long before its due date.

Now, here for the book group was a newer edition, softcover with bright white pages. After reading it cover to cover, I realized my assumptions about it and its concepts of leisure had been all wrong. Pieper, a twentieth-century German philosopher, published this book in 1948 after having first delivered portions of it as two lectures in 1947, just after the end of World War II. He wasn't concerned with shoring up an eroding cultural foundation by advancing geometry and calculus or filling museums with textiles or tools of scientific discovery. Neither did he care about Caribbean cruises and hammocks and umbrella drinks, or rounds of golf or dinner for four at eight. Here was a man pleading with a world of people whose noses were to the grindstone rebuilding businesses, homes, and lives destroyed by the war. Eyes on the job, all hands on deck, preached the day's motivational speakers, betting on productivity and utility to calm the turbulence. In contrast, Pieper pleaded: "pierce the canopy" that work forms over your life and transcend "the work-a-day world." Allow "the totality of existing things to come into play: God and the World," he wrote.

Why this message, this urgency?

To be human.

Start in the world and go up, urged Pieper. True leisure is "a condition of the soul." True leisure is stillness, contemplation, passivity, receptivity, celebration, worship, wonder, mystery, and grace. A Sabbath intervention. These are words I can wrap myself in and relax with. Find, grab hold of, hang on to, defend to the last, this reflective posture, I tell myself, and you find the canopy's needed spear.

A unique joy erupts from the split second transition between work and freedom from work, that moment when the school bell rings and spring break is here at last, or when you walk away from your assigned post and toward the bag packed for a weekend away. In that moment, it is as if the stone has been rolled away in the nick of time and you move and breathe and live again. Work, rush, work; then the cycle of restoration turns, toward freedom, toward play. "Joy is play's intention," wrote Peter Berger, and when joy emerges, time in the playful universe becomes eternity. Gather the bottled water, the sunscreen, the camera. My time in Barcelona ended with a free day.

There had been Casa Battló, a multi-story home, now museum, designed and refurbished between 1904 and 1906 by Modernista architect Antonio Gaudí, whose work is everywhere in Barcelona. Casa Battló's arcs of natural wood and shades of blues, greens, and purples float you on imaginary water. Not a single straight line in the entire place, said the tour guide. The beauty of Gaudí's signature mosaic tiles add into and become a whole so infinitely more beautiful than the sum of its parts that you're left wondering whether to zoom in or out.

There had been Gaudí's Parc Güell with its mosaic iguana at the entrance, the famous mosaic bench undulating like waves on a patio overlooking the city toward the Mediterranean, its tiles with their splashes of cerulean and periwinkle like the sea, pools of yellow like the sun, moons of white. In a pavilion under a ceiling of mosaic starbursts, a classical flautist played Mozart.

There had been the Temple Expiatori de la Sagrada Família, a cathedral built of stone the color of sand, on which Gaudí worked the last 43 years of his life, and where he lived in an on-site studio his last year before being killed, as the story goes, by a tram on his way to Mass. The cathedral's construction, being far from finished at the time, continued in his absence but according to his plan. At the west side entrance, the Passion Façade, stands a sculpture of Christ roped to a pillar, his sunken body slashed by 40 strokes, and above the door a naked stone Christ hangs on a cross. Inside, multi-branched pillars planted like trees rise up to a ceiling that resembles a top-down view of sunflowers, their open faces shining, stained glass glowing in the distance. At the east side's Nativity Façade, the cathedral's stone explodes its sleek reserve into an outburst of detail and filigree: Mary and the baby marking the exit high above the doors; trumpeting angels, palms, and tortoises; the tree of life; a pinnacle mounded with stone fruit—red, green, yellow. Higher still, towers too wild to count. The great architect reportedly delighted in the first tower's completion and "how that spear joins heaven and earth."

There had been the waterfront, I barefoot in the sand, then a boat ride around the harbor, telling myself while afloat to feel, feel the water's buoyancy, the spray of salt, the cool moisture dampening first mouth, then throat, then lungs. "And I will put breath in you," wrote the prophet Ezekiel, "and you will come to life." Breathe deep, deep, and deep again.

There had been a meal under a white umbrella at a sidewalk café, a street musician singing a Frankie Valli hit, "You're just too good to be true / Can't take my eyes off of you," and passing a hat for her pay.

There had been the Gothic cathedral, where other tourists like me wandered and looked, seeking respite from sightseeing's push, where men and women went about their business lighting candles and praying in the pews. A woman knelt in a confessional booth, her varicosed calves and feet extending from under the booth's door, the hem of her faded print dress brushing the floor's cold stone. From beyond the nave, the cloisters called, an interstice vibrant with magnolias and palms, cool with shade and water.

I imagine the pilot walking down the aisle once the plane reached cruising altitude and making a quick study of those he was responsible to transport. Could he spot the passengers with a need for Sabbath? A need for transcendence and beauty? He must have seen crosses on chains draped across necks, a yarmulke or two. Maybe my palm lay open, and he saw the prayer bead ring. I imagine him rushing back to his microphone eager to speak a poetic word to his passengers who yearned for something more.

In C. S. Lewis's *The Last Battle*, there is a scene in which dwarves sit in a sunny open field yet all the while believe themselves to be sitting huddled in a pitch-black stable. So blinded were they by the limited reality they perceived, they could not see things as they really were. Pieper, referencing Aquinas, wrote that to be fulfilled is to have "the whole order of real things be registered in our soul," the full plenum—world without end—through which we travel, live, move, and have our being.

To be part of it all, with the spear of reflection rising up through is the integrated transcendent life for which I long. I yearn, not for the accoutrements of a tourist with a free day in a foreign city, but for the inner equipping of freedom and play, time for my soul to lift and expand to all that is, even while on the path of work. I want a place at the table where data meets humanity. I want to sing while collecting my pay.

I think of Binx, the protagonist in Walker Percy's *The Moviegoer*, as he paused before leaving for work to look at the items he had removed from his pockets the night before—wallet, notebook, pencil, keys, handkerchief, and a slide rule. He saw them as clues and realized a search had begun. I think of the feasting and storytelling between battles and voyages in Homer's *Odyssey*. I think of Tolstoy's Levin as he walked his fields and surveyed his farm while contemplating matters of faith. I think of Moses turning his head from his sheep and toward the bush that burns, shedding his shoes.

I think of Gaudí in the thin space between work and Mass.

Miles and miles from French airspace, the alarm sounds and I rise up from my mattress, place my feet on the hardwood floor, raise a shade and see sun or clouds, turn a knob and walk over the door's threshold. The furnace kicks on, warm air shooting through the vents, the smell of dust at its start. I sip hot coffee with cream from a pottery mug, steam rising. The refrigerator motor hums. Outside my front door, rush hour traffic builds. I sink my hands into hot soapy water and lift out a ceramic bowl or two, stainless steel forks and spoons, and place them on a wooden draining board. A plane booms overhead. Suds wash my face, my hair and skin. I dress in cotton or wool or rayon and slip into leather shoes and pick up a glass perfume bottle and spray a botanical essence on my wrists and neck. My back leans into the chair's cushioned support and my feet push against the floor to scoot chair to desk. My fingers find the keyboard. My eyes see the clock and my shoulders tense.

Work buckles me in and pulls the strap tight. In the margin of a notebook, in seconds stolen from the project at hand, I've scribbled the words, *Brain deep deep down*, like a message in a bottle, like a ransom note.

God once asked Moses a question that comes to me from time to time, "What is that in your hand?" Moses looked down and saw his fingers wrapped tight around his staff that would soon be a tool for miracles: blood from rivers, frogs from thin air, water from rocks. I hear the question now.

What is in your hand?

The work, which I'm always trying to find my way through, breathe through, hold back, finish, master.

What is in your hand?

Olive wood prayer beads, a dangling cross.

What is in your hand?

A phrase, an image: *Pierce the canopy.* The pilot's words: *We are still in French airspace.*

I roll back my fingers and see in my palm the alchemy of truth: the suffocating canopy of work, the need to pierce it, the pull of something more, the relief of turning toward the window, spar-kling like a rhinestone stud, and letting it work its reorienting magic. *God of grace and mercy.* See the heavens—deep and wide—through which we soar; see the plane in peripheral vision as it frames the window; see the fields, mountains, and coastline, the people shaped from clay and eager to live.

Looking up and out, I wonder what God had hoped to see looking down. I lift my face and wave.

EIGHT
Witness

ON SEEING EACH OTHER

Images swish past the still point of our eyes in their sockets, this movable hub of existence. Front and center as you move, or there, out of the corner of your eye. Pick a place, any place, even or especially the workplace, and pause. "Eyes see better when guided by love," wrote Pieper.

For whom and for what have we been assigned the role of witness?

Back then, most days as I walked from the lab to the bus, I carried with me no special image, just more of the same: racks of lavender and red top tubes of blood; empty test tubes and cuvettes, gleaming glass and plastic, waiting to be filled from the tip of a pipette; shelves of bottled chemicals; machines that spun or measured or both; a row of microscopes lined up on a counter; a chair on wheels in front of each. News for someone waited under a microscope lens; why was the news so often bad? Two decades before the millennial turn and most things in this hospital laboratory proceeded in a routine process and could be grossly simplified in summary. Step One: start with blood or other body fluid. Step Two: look at it (proceed to Step Five) or add chemicals (proceed to Step Three). Step Three: measure the reaction. Step Four: record the measurement. Step Five: report what you see or find.

Every afternoon, I took the bus home from the southeast corner of Williams Park, the hub for St. Petersburg's limited bus system. The square-block green space was a magnet for old people who were lonely or poor—or both—many of whom lived in the surrounding residential retirement hotels. They walked along its sidewalks and sat on its palmetto-bordered green benches. Across the street from the park, on the northeast corner of 1st Avenue and 3rd Street North, sat Maas Brothers department store, where I had worked during my senior year of high school and vacations home from college.

One afternoon on the walk to Williams Park and the bus, I carried with me the image of a little boy and his doctor. The little boy was one of those to get bad news from under the microscope. A lifetime of pokes and pains boiled down into the few months he'd been in and out of the hospital. The boy was bald already at the age of six from rounds of chemotherapy sent into his blood by Dr. B, who had entered his room earlier that afternoon to force another stainless steel needle into his hip bone.

Only the boy's medical record kept count of how many times before this doctor had biopsied his marrow. Shortly after each biopsy, Dr. B would walk through the doorway of the lab. As soon as we saw him, before he even asked, "Can I see the slide?" we knew to clear a place for him. He'd sit down in a wheeled chair and push with his feet against the floor to scoot himself over close to the microscope. Someone would hand him the freshly stained slide and he'd snap it onto the scope's stage, anchor both his eyes on the eyepieces, swing the low-power objective into place, turn one knob to get the focus right and another knob to move the slide around, stop to squeeze a drop of oil from a bottle onto the slide, swing another objective into place and settle in. Dr. B then knew how good or bad the news. Simple as that. Turning wheels, swinging objectives, rotating knobs; his eyes the still point in the bald boy's topsy-turvy world. He'd get up quickly, thank us, and leave.

Here in the image I carried, the doctor strode into the boy's hospital room. He wore a white shirt and tie, no lab coat or white jacket. The afternoon sun, the room's only light, shone through a window with partially drawn drapes. Behind Dr. B entered his team who would squirt squirt the collected bone marrow into lavender top tubes and onto slides and swish swish the glass slides together to make smears to peer at later under the scope. I was on his team for the first time and was so young at 22 and knew so little about what would happen in that room that my stomach hurt for the pain of the boy and my pain in watching, and I feared I might faint once things got underway.

The boy, lying on the bed, turned and saw his doctor enter. He sprang up, feet on the bed, the mattress bouncing in response. Sunshine reached through the parted drapes to polish his bald head. The boy opened wide his arms, and Dr. B walked right to him, and they wrapped each other tight, the doctor with his curly black hair now shoulder to shoulder with the boy.

Together they swayed, back and forth, back and forth. Back and forth. Now still, but holding. Holding. The boy smiled as if there were never a reason to do anything but. The pain hadn't even started, and I thought if I did indeed faint it might be from the terrible beauty of this sight alone.

How far beyond the threshold of that room did the holy ground extend? As far as the nurses' station or elevator? As far as the first floor or back to the lab? Perhaps, when my shift ended, if I had lit a candle in order to carry the holiness of that moment with me out the hospital's front door and down the front walkway and to the first street corner, the flame's flicker may have shown me divine territory in every direction, accelerating and expanding from a long ago bang.

Toward the end of my junior year in high school, I applied for the one-year position at Maas Brothers in downtown St. Pete. Each of their area stores had a "Teen Board" made up of a representative girl from each high school in its territory. It's not as if this were an advisory board: "Mr. Chairman, we'd like you to consider lowering prices to match today's economic downturn." Or, "Let's form a task force looking into purchasing patterns from design houses using sweatshop labor." No, predictably, the reason for the board was to have a marketing link with the essential high school demographic, which loaded up on shirts and earrings, shoes and purses. Girls on the board modeled for the store and worked in the departments that served high school girls and guys.

Those of us vying for these positions sat on couches and chairs inside the doorway of the large conference room where the interviews were held. Did we remember the advice of our mothers, to cross our legs only at the ankles? To keep our knees together, back straight, shoulders down, and head high? We watched the girls ahead of us as they conversed with their interviewers. We eyed each other, mentally comparing weight, hairstyles, outfits, and complexion.

When my name was called, I moved to the open position next to one of two interviewers, a well-dressed woman with dark hair and impeccable make-up. In response to one of her questions, I hit pay dirt when I told her I had recently fallen in love with the work of impressionist painter Claude Monet after seeing it for the first time at the Art Institute of Chicago, and one painting in particular had knocked me off my feet. Monet studied light. The interviewer smiled broadly and nodded; she was nuts about Monet also. She bent her head down and made a notation on her paper.

Florida afternoons are hot, so hot, and once the sun leeches out air conditioning's residual chill, unneeded layers, even lab coats, must be shed. I quickly took mine off and draped it across an arm. In the not too distant future, nobody working in a lab would be wearing or carrying a worn lab coat into the outside world, but would be depositing it into a bin at the door destined for sterilization. Even as I walked, researchers across the world were leaning over desktops scribbling out early reports of the mystery disease that ravages the immune system. We didn't know this yet, however, and so cared more about stains than germs. Sometimes blood splashed on the white coat, but if you doused it first with hydrogen peroxide and then held it under a rush of cold water, the blood cells burst wide open upon the perma-press cotton and the iron-red hemoglobin washed away.

At the end of the hospital's block and after the first right turn, like a magnet pulling a needle true north, the two-story residential retirement hotel next to the alley up ahead turned my head to look, same as the afternoon before, and the afternoon before that. White with green trim and a big front porch. Like

most of St. Pete's downtown retirement hotels, you would think
it was just a house if it weren't for the sign out front. A high
school friend lived there, a boy of short-lived boyfriend status.
His parents owned and ran the residence. All I'd ever seen of it
was the inside of a back entryway, part of the kitchen. What
went on in there, I didn't exactly know. I imagined the boy's
mother doing acts of kindness, such as curling the hair of her
female residents, combing it just so. Like her husband and all
their relatives of that generation, she was from a country across
the sea and along the Mediterranean. I'd met her only a few
times. Kind and subdued, sad and melancholic, dressed in black
is how I remembered her, as if she were in some sort of constant
mourning, and maybe she was. I once went to a family wedding,
that of a cousin of the boy. When the extended family gathered
at the front of the church to rotate in and out of poses, they
called to me sitting alone in a pew, "Come, be in the pictures."
I tried to politely refuse, but they persisted and I relented. These
years later as they flip the pages of their wedding album, do they
stop to narrow their eyes and wonder about the girl with the
blond hair and green eyes, "Who is she?"

This retirement hotel and others along my path to the bus
were not like the retirement residences that enjoyed waterfront
views of Tampa Bay a few blocks to the east or the Gulf of Mexico a few miles to the west. They were estranged third cousins
twice-removed to the retirement communities tourists saw pic-
tured on billboards when driving into Florida on I-75 just after
the welcome stations with the free orange juice, or when perusing
Florida's glossy lifestyle brochures. I can't be sure, but I suspect the
hotels were filled with seniors who forgot to do their retirement

planning or who were left alone or behind by spouses or children. The boyfriend dreamt of living far from this place, in a house with an ocean in its backyard on which boats might sail.

The teen board job did not have us swimming in the deep end of life, but splashing and kicking in the shallow. There would be time enough ahead for waters to deepen. That happens without even moving. You step into the shallow water of the Gulf, for example, up to your ankles and just stand there and the water runs in over your feet and out again, the currents passing, swishing and spinning the sand. The sand sucks out from under you and swirls over your toes and the curve of your instep and your ankles, and before you know it the ground sinks and the water rises and you're in deeper.

For now, though, there was the bridal fashion show in the store auditorium, frosted with white satin and lace. A show in Tampa sponsored by Seventeen Magazine. A center layout in the Sunday paper. We clothed ourselves from the latest fashion shipments and twirled through the store's restaurant at the height of lunchtime dining. On Saturdays, we stepped and pivoted, stepped and pivoted on a stage in the high school girl's department while records spun.

We had keys to an office with a desk and fashion magazines, a couch and soft lighting. We posed for ads in our school newspapers. There were no limits to the clothes we could wear if we were content to wear them for just three minutes and give them back. I remember powder-blue satin and a nautical striped knit and a batik cotton print. They weren't what we went home with or to, however, or could select from when groggy and wishful after a night of sleep and dreams.

I turned east and walked three blocks on a sidewalk that cut through lawns thick with the thatch of Florida crab grass. I passed more residential retirement hotels and the masonry South-side homes perched on their latticework foundations where cockroaches and palmetto bugs scurried underneath. At 3rd Street South, the path headed north, passing Central Avenue where the street name changed to 3rd Street North, and continued on to Williams Park and the bus idling at the curb.

Many afternoons, a fish odor permeated the bus. Not the appetizing smell of batter-fried shrimp or grilled tuna, but something raw and rotten. It lingered and mixed with the heat and humidity that rushed in whenever the doors opened and with the moldy air conditioner smell when the doors closed again. Its source had been a mystery. Then one day, while I was sitting on the bus and waiting for it to pull away from the curb, a pair of shoes moved through my peripheral vision. Bloodstains and fish scales speckled their leather surface. My eyes followed the shoes, attached to legs, attached to a torso, moving to the back of the bus. A man turned to take a seat, and I saw across his front the residue of the day's work in a fish market. From then on, if the bus smelled like fish, I knew he was there.

"Excuse me, sir," I longed to ask him, holding my lab coat in my lap. "Why don't you take off that apron before getting on the bus? Then see how we would smile at you; sit next to me if you want. Untie the knot behind your neck, roll the smeary mess into a ball, and stuff it into a plastic bag. So easy!"

I think of my father and his good smell when he left for work in the morning and when he came home, too. Soap, shampoo, and aftershave all mixed together in a way that told me all is well, and he intended for it to stay that way. He always wore a crisp shirt my mother ironed, a tie with a careful knot, a suit or sports coat.

He never took the bus, but opened his car door, got in, backed it out of the driveway, and sped off to work. Pens stood ready in his shirt pocket and a slide rule in his briefcase.

My father grew up working on farms: driving tractors, feeding pigs, and milking cows. "Take those smelly things off!" I imagined my grandmother saying to him when he came in the kitchen door, then just a kid with sweat and animal on him.

I might have asked the fish guy in a gentle voice, "Did you never have someone love you by showing you this is how we do things?" Maybe he worked at a fish market down by the pier, or at the bait house where you could buy a bucket of herring to feed the pelicans, or at a four-star restaurant serving the Gulf Coast's finest seafood.

Sometimes we worked behind the scenes at the real fashion shows starring the professional models and the designer clothing—the shows at the Hilton for charities or the shows to introduce a new season's clothing. A model would finish her runway walk, race to her dressing area, and stand still. I would unclasp the belt, unzip the dress, free her arms from its sleeves, and pull it down, or wiggle a neck hole around and over her made-up face and hair-do. Up with a new dress, around the neck a new gold chain, clip clip dangling and glittering earrings. Slip on a new pair of heels. Pat or puff or smooth her hair. Turn her around and push her off again in search of a new round of gasps and applause at the sheer beauty of the combination of her and her ensemble.

Meanwhile across the street, Doris worked in the basement at Maas Brothers. It had been three years since I worked my last

shift, but I knew she was still there. Sometimes instead of catching the bus home after work, I crossed the street and went in
to buy something or look around. There she would be, walking
up the stairs from the basement or riding the escalator to the
second or third floors, carrying a bag of money to close out her
register or merchandise for shipping or alteration. I see her, but
she never sees me.

When I was an employee, I usually worked in the juniors department, selling clothes I was tempted to buy with my discount
and in listening range of the records—Elton John, Carly Simon,
Boz Scaggs—we played on the turntable in the stock room. But
often, personnel floated me to other departments. Sometimes it
was stationery and books, where I helped the woman who always
dressed just so and who sipped her morning cup alone at the
counter in the first floor coffee shop. Sometimes it was men's
underwear—what did I know of boxers or briefs?—sometimes
shoes or linens. For an entire summer it was the tailor shop, where
women hunched over their sewing machines and the man with a
five-part French name, so regal it sounded as if he should have
presided over the Louvre instead of standing red-faced in bursts
of steam, worked at a standing iron press.

Sometimes I worked with Doris in the basement—the bar-
gain basement, where the smell and economies were different than
along Beach Drive on the bay a few blocks to the east, or in the
store's floors one through three. Above us were the cosmetic and
fragrance counters where Chanel N°5 and Estée were released in
bursts on women's pulse points and carried through the store's
ventilation system to other departments where their musk mixed
with the aroma of shoe leather and jewelry metals and brewed

coffee. Above us were the evening formals and bridal gowns. The restaurant's balcony overlooked the first floor and served fresh seafood and salads on chopping boards garnished with paper umbrellas. You could buy neckties from an elegant woman with a French accent or ask for Lenox china and Waterford goblets to be boxed and sent anywhere. Chocolates waited behind glass.

In the basement, Doris helped customers who scrounged for bargains. She always wore a cotton, buttoned-up blouse and a skirt gathered in soft folds under a waistband. One day an elderly woman with a neglected look about her came to the counter to return a well-worn purse. The woman tipped it upside down, dumping its contents on the counter: used tissues, a tube of lipstick, a coin pouch, random scrap papers, a worn bus transfer, pens, loose nickels, and pennies.

"See how it's not right," she said, pointing inside to the acetate lining littered with tissue shreds and marred by coin scrapes. Doris and I peered in and saw nothing other than hard wear.

"No, I can't give you money back for this purse," said Doris, "It looks like you've been using it a long time." She added that the store had never even carried that purse.

"Get me the manager."

The manager arrived, sophisticated in his gray suit, white shirt, and dark tie, no doubt purchased in the men's department on the first floor, probably from the French woman who knew her ties. He roamed the floor for just these kinds of moments.

"How can I help you?" he asked the customer.

The woman repeated her story. Doris and I watched him as he listened, confident he would talk sense to the woman and vindicate Doris.

"Do you have your receipt?"

"No."

Aha, here was the point on which he would resolve the matter—a simple default to the rules of the game. No receipt; no refund.

"Do you remember how much you paid for it?" the manager asked, a conciliatory tone beginning to ribbon through his words.

"Fifteen dollars."

"Give her 15 dollars," he said to Doris.

"We're sorry for your trouble," he said to the customer.

Doris, nearly swallowed now by the gathered skirt and buttoned blouse, opened the cash register, removed the cash, and handed it to the customer. With her hand, she slid the purse contents across the counter and into a bag. She handed this also to the woman, who then—head high—turned and walked away.

"It's always easier to keep a current customer than find a new one," the manager told us. Then he too walked away.

Sometimes we stood like mannequins on a platform at the top of the escalators between the first and second floors. The rules were simple: Don't move. When someone passed closely by or stood in front of you, the bar rose higher. No breathing except for the slightest lift from your gut if you got desperate. Keep your shoulders level, chin up, and face straight ahead. Blink only when the viewer looked away from your face. Ignore the burn of dry eyes; command your blink and swallow reflexes. As people swish past your line of vision, moving between escalators and departments or in and out of the restaurant, keep your eyes wide open but still.

One day a little girl stands and watches my face. She tries to catch my eye, but I can't let her see that I see her. She wants to see that she's been seen because then she'll know I'm real. I hold steady despite the burn in my unblinking eyes and the temptation to look at her. She tires of the game and gives up on being seen and instead, examines me closely from several angles. Out of the corner of my eye I see her jaw drop. She tugs at her mother's sleeve, points, and says, "Look, mom, that one has a zit!"

How could my eyes not blink at that, the corners of my mouth not twitch at the humor, my lungs not expand in relief at the illusion burned through? A blemish, one among oh so many, and the humanity there all along breaks through.

I see; you see; both of us, all of it, real.

Meanwhile, a few blocks away, the dreaming boy's mother went about her duties. As I waited for the bus to pull away from the park, and Doris climbed the stairs up from the basement, and the fish guy sat down for maybe the first time all day, the hotel proprietress stood in an upstairs bedroom, dressed in black, a small comb in her hand. A woman with gray hair who hoped to salvage a perm sat on the bed in front of the window. Perhaps the woman had rested earlier that afternoon on a green bench in the park. Perhaps she was the one who years earlier had returned the purse to Doris; but no matter. The proprietress gently combed each curl urging it to bend and wave, teasing when necessary. They glanced out the window at nothing much. A seafood stew simmered in the kitchen, and she would soon put down the comb and go set the table for her guests. She'd light a candle. I imagine this scene and believe it to be true.

NINE
Two-Part Invention

ON THE PRACTICE OF DIVIDED ATTENTION

I have invented a driver who stopped his car next to the cab in which I rode on the backed-up freeway entrance ramp and did a double take at the sight of the flute in the cab driver's hands. He looked inside and saw a passenger, eyes closed, resting her head against the back seat's top arc. Maybe it occurred to him that this was only a cabbie's ploy for tips, but he turned off his radio, rolled down his window, and listened just the same.

I've invented this driver because I want a witness to the music. When I was a little girl, my parent's Ford sedan had no radio. Stopped at a red light next to any car with music streaming out through an open window, my older brother and I would look at each other, smiling and laughing at our good fortune to snatch a taste of what lay beyond our own four doors. We imagined ourselves in a car that wasn't ours, going who knows where, singing along to music and even snapping our fingers to the beat as we went.

We travelers are at the mercy of traffic, and Chicago traffic had stopped on the Foster Avenue entrance ramp to the Kennedy. Young and in college, I was headed home for a break. Next stop, O'Hare, could be 15 minutes or an hour away. The memory of my cabbie's appearance isn't clear beyond his dark hair, clean shave, and olive complexion. He must have hoisted my suitcase into the trunk when he picked me up at the dorm, a slate-blue hardcover Samsonite with light blue satin lining. The suitcase had been my grandmother's, then my mother's, then mine, and it had been to places I had not. No doubt I'd sat on it; I always had to, my weight pushing the over-stuffed sides to meet before the case would close and the two latches click shut. At that age I was smack in the middle of planning a life, hoping for a career, trying to figure out if I could indeed have it all, wondering and worrying about many things. I wanted to fly but instead was in a cab in a traffic jam with 1,200 miles of airspace between departure and arrival. From the front seat came a flash of silver, and the driver lifted a flute to his mouth.

Into the traffic, a space opened for the music to fill.

The plans, the rush, the plane up ahead vanished. In this cab were stillness and beauty. Around the driver, no piccolos or clarinets joined in, no trumpets or trombones, no conductor led the way. The man at his steering wheel played his flute for seconds or minutes until traffic began again to move, and he stopped and placed the flute back on the seat.

I asked him about his playing after we merged onto the northbound Kennedy. He said he did it for his customers.

They are stressed and anxious, he said; my music brings them peace.

I expect that the flute rolled into the seat's crack where it waited within reach, in one piece, ready to play again. When traffic moves, there is no time to separate the parts and press them into a velvet-lined case; when traffic stops and it is time again to play, there is not a moment to waste reassembling. Alongside the flute would be his logbook where he recorded his miles and times, passengers and destinations. Maybe a grocery list too and a check waiting to be cashed.

To be sure, he picked up and played the flute later that day and the next, again and again, for there is no lack of traffic jams or anxiety on these streets.

Ralph Waldo Emerson wrote, "But do your work, and I shall know you." So here is a question: the cab or the flute—which was the cabbie's work?

On yellowed college-ruled paper, in bright blue ink and the kind of loop-de-loop handwriting that betrays an earnestness just short of maturity, are pages of notes I took long ago from a professor's talk on career advice: "Nothing is for positive in life and thus any of these—money, prestige—may be lost overnight.... If one chooses a career in the context of a calling, so much worry is eliminated.... Your calling encompasses everything you are as a person. Use every part of yourself!... Study to explore the great infinite capacity which lies within yourself." At that age, there were so many things that one could yet be, but driving a cab was a job I knew I'd never have. Give me a job with glass beakers, Bunsen burners, and petri dishes, a job of science that gets my hands dirty.

In the cracks between college biology and chemistry classes and labs, I took piano lessons from the music department for

liberal arts credit. The practice rooms were off a single gray cor-
ridor in the basement of the music building. The sign-up sheet
hung on a wall at the bottom of the stairs. I knew I didn't belong
there, even though the lessons granted me permission, and so I
wrote my name in time slots when no one was looking, stealing an
hour a day from those who were making music their livelihood.

My piano teacher assigned scales and selections from an as-
sortment of music books. I remember Mendelssohn's *Songs without
Words* and Bach's two-part *Inventions.* In high school, I had started to learn these inventions and was happy to revisit them. Each
hand, left and right, seemed to have its own business, which suited
me. Thrilled me even. The voice of the left hand did not bow to a
single grand melody delivered by the voice of the right. Each hand
played its part, which was a whole in itself, dipping and weaving
and synced in time against the other hand's part until both parts
ended in a paced rush on a single, harmonizing beat.

I am paging through the old music book, its gold cover long
gone, my teacher's handwriting here and there, marking fingering
or dates by which to finish. The introduction tells us that Johann
Sebastian Bach composed these tutorial-like pieces for his students so that, in his own translated words, they could be shown
"a plain Method of learning not only to play clean in two Parts,
but likewise in further Progress to manage three *obbligato* Parts well
and correctly, and at the same time not merely how to get good
Inventions [ideas], but also how to develop the same well." Look
at the scores and what you see in parallel tracts is a series of
ascents—higher and higher—then descents before rising again.
Mordents and reversed mordents could keep two or three fingers
trilling forever if there was no need to keep time. To earn my final

credit, I came up from the basement practice rooms for a recital. Washed and scrubbed from dissections, the Krebs cycle neatly memorized, Bunsen burner extinguished, qualitative and quantitative analyses of every sort accounted for in my blue-gridded laboratory notebook, I seated myself at a piano on a stage and played Mendelssohn's "Agitation," a six-page piece played *presto agitato* in the key of B-flat major.

Emerson wrote, "Do your work, and you shall reinforce yourself." Which work shall this be? Here is one work, and there alongside it or simultaneously just beyond it is another work. You pick something, and then you pick something else to put into that first something, and then you pick something else to put into that other something in a vocational *mise en abyme*, like one Russian doll nested inside the other. But the metaphor fails because there can be no predesigned, linear stacking.

Glory be to the Father, and to the Son, and to the Holy Ghost. A minister I know thinks that we should raise our voices in doxology—word or song—far more often than we do. *As it was in the beginning, is now and ever shall be.* "Walk around all day humming it," he said with a laugh, a challenge in his smiling eyes.

Poet and essayist Adam Zagajewski tells the story of being at a chamber music concert in the courtyard of a Tuscan palace that had once been a monastery. In response to a quartet's playing of Mozart, the audience gave only sparse applause. Troubled at this inadequate response to the music, he launched a defense of ardor, winding through examinations of irony, intellectual poverty, and the loss of the sacred before landing on the concept of *metaxu.*

The word traces back to the Greek word "metaxy" in Plato's *Symposium* and means one or more variations of "between." The word links two disparate points: earth and heaven, seen and unseen, beginning and never-endingness, human and divine. Zagajewski suggests that perhaps those who could barely muster a clap when confronted with the music had difficulty moving in the space between quotidian and transcendent, point A to B—or B to A, depending on one's starting perspective. Like looking through a pair of binoculars, the trick is to look boldly, one eye on the left and the other on the right, and see what you can see when the two vision fields overlap and the images merge.

Bifocal glimpses of reality come along all the time. Three-and-a-half hours into the flight of Apollo 8, astronauts Frank Borman and Jim Lovell—the first humans ever to be pulled into the gravitational field of a non-earth force—looked back at the view as their spacecraft hurtled up and away. "We see the earth now," said Borman, "almost as a disk." Through the window, the world registered in a glance. Lovell narrated a wide-screen view of Florida and West Africa en route to the far side of the moon. Cape Canaveral in one eye and Gibraltar in the other.

World without end. This doxology ends with a roar through space, from starting note to no end in sight, like a train set in motion long ago that won't be stopped. When my sons were little, I told them over and over, "I love you infinity." *Amen.*

My applied science education expanded to include needles and tubes and blood. Our white lab coats crisp and buttoned, my classmates and I sat one day in the laboratory at its black Formica counter. In front of us and standing upright in racks were tubes of our own blood that we had obtained while practicing veni-puncture, the art of drawing blood, on each other. The boxes and boxes of glass microscope slides sealed in cellophane wrap suggested that here would be an extravagance of practice. Our instructor knew this would take awhile to get right.

Start with two slides on the counter: slide one receives the drop of blood; slide two spreads the blood across slide one's surface. We were learning to make "peripheral blood smears," which is a way to prepare blood so that it can be examined on a cellular level under a microscope. Machines can tell you a lot about the blood fed into them—for example, how many platelets it contains, the concentration of hemoglobin, the proportion of different kinds of white blood cells, and even the diameter of its average red blood cell—but only the human eye, trained and open, can both count cells and perceive subtle variations.

Place a drop of blood the size of a small garnet bead on slide one, centered and about half inch from the end. Work fast. Press the narrow edge of slide two against the surface of slide one directly in front of the blood at about a 60-degree angle. Drag it backward until it has passed through almost the entire drop. The blood runs out along the edge in both directions, and just before it reaches across the slide's full width, reduce slide two's angle to about 45 degrees and pull the blood quickly across the length of slide one. The resulting smear looks like a feather if you did it right, dense toward the bottom and center and thinner along the edges.with a feather's characteristic wispy fringe along the top. Under a microscope, there in the fringe but not its edge, is where you'll find cells presenting themselves for examination, single-layered and single file. Make another and another, finish the box, rip cellophane wrap, and finish that box too. Spend the supply. Memorizing facts can be rushed, but developing small motor skills, eye-hand coordination, and muscle memory takes time and practice.

Practice doesn't stop there. Practice staining slides. Practice counting cells. Practice identifying normal and abnormal cells under the microscope. Practice words of taxonomy and description.

Writing this now, years after I last made a smear, I can still feel the movements in my hand. I pick up two index cards loaded with words and press and spread them one against the other, hoping for a fringe, and in my mind's eye they are ready for the scope.

I have recently read the most beautiful phrase: "*a beholding that ascends.*" The thing beheld is a bridge. *Metaxu.* The gaze draws you up.

Pavel Florensky, a late nineteenth-century Russian scientist and ordained Orthodox priest, wrote that phrase. Florensky's dream was to be a monk, but rather than have him waste his scientific training, his bishop refused to give him the required blessing. Instead of a life of monastic contemplation, he reported for daily duty as head of research in a plastics plant and to university lecture halls where he taught physics and engineering wearing his cassock, cross, and priest's cap while under the watchful eye of Kremlin authorities. Eventually, he ended up on a train to a Siberian gulag, where he died four years later, but not before he wrote those words—*a beholding that ascends*—and more about the experience of seeing Orthodox religious icons, mediators between earth and heaven.

Not long ago, I read advice by the unknown author of *The Cloud of Unknowing*: pick a word and hold it in your mind against the push of all words or impressions to the contrary. I like the idea of a word helping steer one's course. Choosing ahead of time that this is what I'll be about. I am practicing *Behold* as that word that steers me. *Behold* as a modus operandi, a way to witness, but more. In that gaze, to dwell, to linger. To hold. Open your hands and cup them together; receive what is given without dropping a crumb; pay attention and wait. Who can imagine all the places from which data come, pointing the eye to space beyond and back again? Julian of Norwich saw in a hazelnut all that was ever made.

I am placing blank index cards and a pad of paper alongside my work, in the cracks between journal articles on blood gone wrong, PowerPoint slides on hepatitis, and meeting notes on bone cancer. For seconds or minutes, I am stopping the words that are usually in my head during a workday—*faster, harder, better, longer*—and practicing writing about something other than disease. Practicing building bridges with words from seen to unseen and back again. Practicing seeing bridges already here. Practicing crossing the bridges found.

The experts say wholeheartedness is a key to fulfillment in work. Give yourself wholly, they urge. In a contrarian act of willful unwholeheartedness, I allow a fault line. To operate on one level here and another level there, is this not the same as a woman nursing one child while reading to another? Or perhaps this is wholeheartedness after all, but with a directional force that lies in another plane.

Call it a proof-of-concept trial, the endpoint being some measure of meaning, an invention yet to be and practiced even now.

In the long line of progress from what is unknown to known, from a need unmet to met, this sort of trial is an early step. You prove one thing and it takes you to a next step you may or may not have predicted.

Next to my computer hangs a copy of Andrei Rublev's Holy Trinity icon, which reflects the story of Abraham's hospitality from Genesis. Three figures are seated at a round table. Two of the figures are robed in brilliant blue, and the third in gold. They are seated at the nine, twelve, and three o'clock positions. On the table is a gold chalice. You look at the icon, *see it,* and the image with the table's open space at the six o'clock position invites you to step up to the scene and take a seat.

The wheel that swings the bell in the tower down the street begins to rotate. The arc of rising bronze jolts as the hanging steel clapper strikes the twin wall that follows behind, starting the vibrations that gush through the bell tower openings. The waves of sound soak the sky, flow through trees, roll across rooftops, drip down walls, seep under door frames.

The morning is new and I am reading from the Old Testament, my eyes moving left to right across the lines, top to bottom down the page, covering one word after another with their gaze, and here now is a chapter break. My thoughts meet the page at the white space, and I realize that my mind and my eyes had split almost from the start, my mind focused as it is so often on work and the tasks of yesterday and what will come today.

I am retracing the visual path, right to left, bottom to top, and beginning again. *Behold.* There is Elijah at the widow's home; the jar of flour that was not used up and the jug of oil that did not run dry; the widow's son ill and not breathing; Elijah with the boy in his arms, crying out to the Lord; Elijah stretched out on the boy, flesh on flesh. And now, the boy without breath breathes. He lives. This drama of life and love had been before my eyes without even the pause due a beautiful peach.

With brain busy and eyes dazed, what else have I missed?

May the Lord make him to live was Elijah's prayer and, likewise, I pray for myself.

TEN
Break

ON BUFFERS

ise up and live. A command, a promise. Years ago I fell into the habit of saying this to myself at the moment of throwing back the covers. Today it is bravado after predawn restlessness. The day had awakened too early to birdsong. The silent alarm clock glowed red: 4:30 AM.

Urgent, insistent. In recent mornings, the backyard robins have started their choral work an hour or two before the sky's darkness gives way to light. The late-March air moves between the spruce and lilac's branches and carries the song through the open windows in my bedroom. I wake up. Is this their mating song? A guerrilla tactic against intruders? I could consult an authoritative source but instead prefer to imagine their whistling fills them with verve sufficient to descend later in the day to the grass and dirt of my lawn to poke for worms—their work. Or maybe it is simply joy, an I-just-gotta-dance preprogrammed outburst. Sometimes you can't distinguish work energy from any other vibrant energy, life-giving as work often can be, the kind of work that triggers the whistle as opposed to the kind that makes me clench my jaw, reach for the Advil, and murmur frustrated words in my mind and occasionally voice them to the empty room, the kind of work that grounds me to the chair from which I could see the robins perching on the branches of the spruce and lilacs if I would ever turn to the window and look.

A perfect storm is gathering. Three work projects that were to be spread over several months are rolling in behind schedule or ahead, threatening to crash over my desk at the same time and to pull me under in the process. I've been lying in bed, conjuring up a mental calendar, scrolling its squares over and over, trying different schedule scenarios, but there are never enough squares.

Six AM and light now fills the sky, the muted light of an early cloudy day. *Rise up and live.* I slip a sweater over flannel pajamas and don my glasses. Isak Dineson wrote in one of her *Seven Gothic Tales*, "Coffee, according to the women of Denmark, is to the body what the word of the Lord is to the soul." I am in need of both but coffee first. It gurgles and steams in its maker.

From the second shelf in my kitchen cupboard, the pottery mug I bought last fall catches my eye. It is the color of Lake Superior on a cold day, frothy green, with waves of brush strokes dividing the froth with currents of gray and white. Its inside is a darker mottled green and gray, like gravel under a wave as it flattens out on the shore. Into the mug, I pour the coffee and cream.

In a kind of moment I've come to think of as guerrilla leisure—a covert and unconventional small assault on the pressure of labor—I make myself pause and feel the pottery's warmth in my hands. I sit down with my journal and write about the early morning fitfulness. Like an artist who paints what's in front of her, I add a description of the mug.

The mug has no handle, which is what attracted me when I lifted it off the shelf at the art gallery. It's a goblet really—a chalice—but nearly all bowl with the barest foot. Its body, slightly narrower in the middle than at the top or bottom, felt right seated inside the curve of my hand. Holding it in the gallery, I imagined how the pottery would feel when warmed by coffee or tea on a cold day. It would remind me of the lake and the weekend I bought it and the need for break as it sat on the table next to my notebooks or the desk alongside the computer. What I didn't consider is that the filled pottery would so efficiently conduct the liquid's heat, burning my hands without an insulating napkin wrapped around the outside.

The October before, a friend and I had driven 160 miles northeast up Interstate 35 to Duluth, a city that sits on the western tip of the largest freshwater lake in the world. Lake Superior, "Gitche Gumee," is a lake so deep and wide that if its basin emptied itself, then three feet of water would cover all of North America; a lake so treacherous that it has swallowed more than 350 ships, including the Detroit-bound *Edmund Fitzgerald* with its 29 men and 26,000 tons of iron ore. Gordon Lightfoot famously sang of the tragedy, "Does any one know where the love of God goes when the waves turn the minutes to hours?"

A weekend's pause from work is what my friend and I had in mind—a mini creative writing retreat. Our plans included nothing more than lunch by the lake, walks along the shore and to the lighthouse, heads bowed over paper or keyboard, and breaks at the coffee shop down the street. A hotel on Canal Park Drive gave us a room with a lake view, two beds, a desk, and a couch.

I bought the mug at Sivertson Gallery, an art gallery across the street from the lake and just northwest of our hotel. The gallery's walls are snow white and the carpet is a deep sea blue. The morning sun from the lake to the east streams in across the "Art of the North": photography, oil and watercolor paintings, jewelry, stone carvings, pottery and ceramics of the North Shore, that strip of shoreline northeast from Duluth to the Canadian border and its surrounding wilderness. Like agates on the shore, the reds, browns, blacks, and greens of the region's iron oxide spread along the display shelves. Like wildflowers along the road, the pinks, blues, purples, and white of the lady's slipper, lupine, bluebell, star thistle, swamp iris, and wild trillium scatter across canvases and prints, across the card rack and jewelry counter.

The gallery's middle section was given over to an art show in celebration of the daily break. *"Behold!"* spilled in black italics across the top of the banner that hung in the window, followed by, "THE MUG," all caps and blue serif, on the line below. The blue continued on the banner's third line, "Celebrate the Break Time Ritual." The banner's graphic was a take-off of Michelangelo's, "Creation of Adam," the Sistine Chapel's centerpiece fresco. The hand of God, the creator, reaches down to touch the hand of Adam, *imago Dei*, reaching up. Their hands connect and the spark of life passes from divine to mortal.

In Sivertson's version, cropped to include only the hands, liberties are taken and a white pottery mug passes from one to the other. Artists from across the country had submitted their creative interpretations of break time. A studio potter in North Carolina made the mug I bought. The sales clerk gave me a copy of his artist statement. "I have made this object with my hands with the intentions of you using it with your hands," he wrote. "Your touch embracing my touch. The direct connection between maker and user."

A tall multi-shelved display unit held porcelain and pottery mugs, short and squat, tall and thin, plain to garish, neutral to fuchsia. Display tables along the sidewall held more mugs, tea sets, teapots, and trays.

Along the wall hung these lines of Eliot's:

> Time for you and time for me,
> And time yet for a hundred indecisions,
> And for a hundred visions and revisions
> Before the taking of a toast and tea.

Early morning clouds break open in a few places and the sky brightens. Rush hour has begun, and the rumble of buses and the swoosh of cars come more frequently now through the open window. A chipmunk that my husband and I have predictably named Chippy takes his usual place on the deck. Only a few days earlier, he had emerged from his winter hibernation and began his early morning contemplative routine. Given the limited lifespan of an average chipmunk in the wild, we realize this is probably not the same chipmunk year after year, but his repeated daily pattern suggests otherwise. Seated and still on the corner of the bench, he fixes his gaze at some point in the backyard. The movements of squirrels or cardinals do not deter him. A few minutes pass, and he pivots to face a slightly different direction and is still again. Soon, the bells in the church tower down the street will ring, a call to pray.

It is Lent, and throughout the season, I have been listening to an online audio meditation offered by the British Jesuits. A woman starts the meditation today in the same way as the others that have come before it—the third week, the second, the first—grounded in time, "Today is the thirtieth of March, in the fourth week of Lent." The focus on now, on today, calms me. Squares of the mental calendar vanish. I have not fallen behind, nor must I jump ahead.

Bells chime seven times, and the cellos and violins begin. Hanno Müller-Brachmann sings an aria from Bach's *St. Matthew Passion*, "*Mache dich, mein Herze, rein.*" *Make my heart pure.* His voice swells, rising in amplitude before falling and rising again. The singing pauses, but the instruments play on while the woman again talks. As if all the time in the world is at her disposal within this 10-minute audio recording, using words slow and paced, she suggests that a pure heart is one that is open to God, surrendered. She pauses, and Müller-Brachman sings again.

Now, a man reads the day's text, a Psalm recalling how the people built the golden calf at the foot of Mount Horeb while waiting for Moses to finish talking to God. Their memories were short; they had forgotten God's splendor and flash. The woman returns and asks a question about our remembering. She pauses again. A pianist plays without hurry. Another question; another pause; the pianist returns. Listening to this synchronized team of speakers, soloist, and pianist—a person has time. All is well, no need to rush. Approaching storms stall before such a shield of calm.

Finally, the woman asks, "What things do I want the grace to be mindful of in the coming day so that I make choices that are good, honorable, and true?" Put like that, with the link between knowing and doing, and between divine and human offerings, it's an interesting question, one I want to think about. The pianist plays again. I write the question in my journal, but its emerging answer is interrupted when a gold email icon appears at the bottom of my computer screen.

The email tells that a man I know died this morning. His liver cancer was diagnosed only two weeks ago. Just over a year ago, this man delayed the start of his retirement to help a small band of people who needed him—a weary group in a dying church. *Come unto me all who are weary and heavy-laden, and I will give you rest.* He said other words from the pulpit, but that is what we heard. To the call of the golf course, he must have whispered again and again, "get thee behind me." If the British woman from the online meditation had asked him her final question, he could have quickly answered, because he must have asked it of himself every day, dying as he did in the pursuit of the good, the honorable, and the true.

Glory be to the Father, and to the Son, and to the Holy Spirit. As it was in the beginning, is now, and ever shall be. With doxology, the meditation ends.

The workday begins. Gone is the time for the grace to be mindful. The phone rings. The phone rings. Emails fly back and forth. I am writing about exercising and food without salt, about sphygmomanometers and blood pressure, about medicines and statistical outcomes and quality of life. The phone rings. The phone rings. Off to the side sits the frothy lake in the mug, coffee cold.

In Duluth, during our writing retreat, I wrote about a Monet painting I first saw long ago. My friend wrote a story about a ship off the coast of Maine. We drank hot tea. We passed a package of red licorice back and forth between us. At dusk, shouts came from outside our hotel room window. Footsteps pounded against asphalt. We looked outside and saw a crowd gathering at the shore. Flashing red lights sped down the narrow lane usually traveled by horse-drawn tourist-laden carriages. We watched for a while, but then made ourselves move away, close the drapes, pray in silence for whatever was happening, and return to our writing. Later that evening, we walked to a restaurant and saw the yellow police tape along the shore. Red lights blinked from the water.

The local news later reported that a man had been crushed against the rocks by his 5,000-pound boat. He couldn't control the boat as it drifted toward the shoreline's black basalt rocks, rocks large enough to require leaps on foot when passing from one to the next, rocks with edges sharp enough to recall the cracking and upheaval of bedrock at their formation. I imagine that a mental picture of basalt piercing his vessel cost him his common sense. He jumped from the boat and stood on rock, pushing against the boat to hold it back and keep it safe. I imagine that only when it was too late, in the minutes that became hours as he watched the rising rocking waves, did he realize that in the contest of human, boat, and rock, the human should never be the buffer against the rock for the boat.

Today I am writing about hearts that pump too hard and hearts that give out, about brains that die when blood is dammed by a clot or released by hemorrhage, about blood that pushes against arteries so fiercely they nearly burst and sometimes do.

～

People are dying of the diseases I get paid to write about, and the world is heating up every which way. It's hard to argue for the importance of wondering about the robins, or mindfully feeling the pottery's warmth, or watching the chipmunk, or listening to the British voices, or writing down a question that remains to be answered. With red lights flashing and cries to resuscitate, my thoughts about a painting and my friend's description of a ship seem to matter not a whit.

Should we not throw out the notebooks and the pens, give back our time of retreat if we could, and take up our positions on the front lines using all of our energies to work tirelessly against all that assails and assaults humankind? Might I better spend my time as billable hours? For my husband and me, there's been an unplanned drop in income—a slash—yet the bills in the mailbox don't abate. The words in my journal won't pay those bills.

The afternoon past peak, I am thinking these thoughts with a tired brain, in need of the grace to be mindful.

Next door, my neighbor Bob is outside working; he has a long obedience to what he grows. When he wants a break, he'll sit in his lawn chair with white and brown woven webbing on a foldable aluminum frame. Sometimes he sits in the shade in his driveway, other times, next to whatever bush or plant he is tending.

The flame under the teapot boils the water for tea. Longing for the pause, the aria's rhythm of rising and falling and rising again, I wrap my hands around the filled chalice.

Behold!

Cupped, still hands; grace in stone, glazed colors of the rolling deep.

Behold!
Holy time frothing; buoy and anchor.
Behold!
Life sparks; a potter's hand circumscribing the space that flames.

More than halfway through my life, I have only just realized that tea is meant to be drunk hot. It is meant to be sipped while seated, hot until the end, and not carried around or forgotten while I work, cooling then zapped and zapped again in the microwave.

When Bob's wife, Leatrice, joins him, they sit together in matching lawn chairs. I've seen him bring the chair out for her, unfold it, and set it on the ground with an extra jiggle and push to make sure it's secure before she sits.

Rain comes as suppertime approaches, the first thunderstorm of the season. The phone rings. The phone rings. I am writing about pressure that mounts, about how to define "too high," about which interventions succeed. Hail bounces on the sidewalk. Emails fly back and forth. *World without end. Amen.*

ELEVEN
Away We Go

ON LONGING FOR ESCAPE (OR IS IT FREEDOM?)

On a weekend afternoon, when perhaps I should have been learning to use Excel or brushing up on getting-things-done strategies, I've instead been reading *Frenchman's Creek*, a novel written in 1941 by Daphne Du Maurier. It's about a woman who nearly runs away with a pirate.

For one dollar at a used book sale, I bought this copy, a 1943 edition from Doubleday. The book has blue cloth boards with blind-stamped author initials on the cover and gold lettering on the spine. Leaving behind a husband and social life, protagonist Lady Dona St. Columb flees her home in seventeenth century London with her two children and their nurse to spend the summer at Navron, their mansion on the coast of Cornwall. Bored with herself and society, weary of street smells and chatter, she sees this as no planned summer vacation but a desperate reset.

My copy has no dust jacket, but the image on the first U.S. edition's jacket shows a solitary woman wearing a dress with a dark bodice and full gathered red skirt, standing on a forsaken, rocky stretch of shore. Heavy gray clouds overhead, she is looking out toward a ship, its sail half down, positioned at the mouth of a narrow creek whose path stretches toward the horizon where light is breaking. Dare I admit this isn't the first time I've read Lady Dona's story? It called to me again from the shelf.

Du Maurier is perhaps best known for *Rebecca*, an earlier novel written in 1938. Alfred Hitchcock made it into a film, winning the Academy Award for Best Picture of 1940. In *Rebecca*, the young female protagonist, who goes unnamed throughout the entire book, is plucked out of her life as a lady's companion and swept away by the rich and debonair Maxim De Winter to his estate, Manderley. Along with the estate comes his secret and his villainous housekeeper, Mrs. Danvers. *Frenchman's Creek* explores a similar theme: exchanging one's life for a different life and the resulting unforeseen consequences. In this later novel, the themes of escape and freedom are urgent. They are the text and subtext on almost every page.

Stories of breaking free are ubiquitous. There's the memoir about the man who left his marriage and his work and moved to California, where he walked the beach and stared at the sky and waves. There's the memoir about the woman who went away to find herself on the opposite coast. There's another memoir about another woman who left it all behind and traveled the world in three acts, and the fictional story of the woman who went for a walk on the beach and just kept walking, never looking back, and the story lines of movies too numerous to count.

And of course, there's the story of near-mythical proportion of how Henry David Thoreau exchanged his life in Concord for two years in a cabin by a pond.

At Navron, Dona quickly learns that in recent months villages along the coast have fallen victim to pirates. Despite the best efforts of local authorities, the pirates evade capture. Yet, Dona discovers their hiding place within a few days of arriving: the ship, sails down, nestled safely in the bend of a creek on her estate. Forget the news stories of modern-day pirates who take hostage innocent shipmen or slaughter vacationing boaters. At first she is captured, but this pirate captain is handsome, a philosopher, and an artist. Most of all, he is French to her English. Rather than becoming his prisoner, she signs on as one of his gang. Not all of her summertime escape features the pirate, however. Dona exchanges her fancy dresses for muslin frocks; she avoids social callers; she spreads blankets on the lawn and watches clouds and butterflies with her children. She becomes tan in the sun, loosens her ringlets, and tucks her hair behind her ears. She walks in the woods and gathers bluebells.

"That guy had way too much time on his hands," my doctor once said about Thoreau. Thoreau, the most celebrated of all escapists and freedom seekers; my doctor, a man who never takes a lunch break and rarely a vacation. I had been reading *Walden* while waiting in the examination room, and my doctor noticed when he entered. He shook his head while making the remark as if to underscore his lack of awe for the iconic figure. In the hallway outside the exam room, his lab tech kept a days-until-retirement clock on her desk for years, and patients could track the countdown every time they sat in her blood-drawing chair.

Robert Richardson's biography of Thoreau begins with a quote from Goethe, "To live within limits, to want one thing...." Anyone with more than a single sense of "what I do" or "should be doing," any person who is juggling more than one ball in the air, no matter how smoothly, has felt the two or more works rub up against each other sufficiently and often enough to start an unmistakable friction. Choose one, name the other a burden, and lay it down. Temptation or call to action? On a duty-cluttered day, Thoreau's life by the pond seems just the ticket, a life in which everything can be put right as easily as moving it all into the sunshine and hosing it down. Is this a longing for freedom, or simplicity, or merely for rest?

Shortly after Dona and the pirate meet, he comes to her mansion, sits in her salon, and sketches her portrait. But she doesn't like what she sees. Dona knows there are two Donas. One is narrow and strained; the other is open and relaxed. My husband and I both know in each other the "vacation face." A couple of days with sunshine and warmth are a prerequisite to its emergence, along with long walks and time on a shore. Vacation face contrasts with the face that is set like flint toward work—mouth pursed, eyes squinted, cheeks tight, forehead furrowed. The vacation face is years younger with eyes bright, skin smooth, and mouth soft. The pirate initially draws the first Dona. He apologizes and rips it up. Later, after the muslin and loose hair have become her routine and they have spent time together such that they are well on their way—predictably—to falling in love, he draws a new likeness of her. This time, he draws the second Dona, and she allows it to hang on his cabin wall.

The pirate talks of a shared blemish between Dona and him: a yearning to escape. Here is the throb du Maurier posits, the throb of what we want versus what is expected of us. What's next? What more is there? Where are we supposed to be because it certainly cannot be where we already are? I wonder how universal this throb is. Even though in this case the means of escape is unjustified— becoming a pirate's mistress and joining his gang, no matter how romantic it sounds to cook over an open fire on a hidden beach, and to fall asleep under the open stars or to the gentle rocking of a ship hidden in a cove—Dona is one of us, imagining greener grass, sensing, hearing, feeling something beyond her given place.

When is this yearning a blemish and when is it a nudge? When is restlessness simply restlessness and when is it divinely breathed?

My head fills with dreams, ideas, and schemes of freedom to be weighed against the movement of the Spirit. Sometimes I've stayed put; sometimes I've made moves. I once quit a job after eight years because I had had enough of that particular workplace's stress. Like a family with a shared virus, my and my coworkers' stomachs hurt when we went to work in the mornings, and I was weary. At the close of that job's final day, my husband and I brought our young sons to their grandparents for the evening and bought take-out salads from a grocery store deli. It was a summer evening, and we ate the salads from their plastic containers, using plastic forks in a pavilion by a lake. Though we wondered how the bills would all be paid, we laughed and laughed.

TWELVE
Summa Laborum II

ON MONEY'S PLACE (A DEBATE)

THE QUESTION

Should money be excluded from a discussion about the meaning in work?

~

REASONS TO ANSWER YES

1. It seems that the counsel of the wise through the ages is to put money in its place and that place is never on top. Treasure in heaven beats a purse on earth.

2. Go to the library or a bookstore, and find the books that comprise the literature of work. Steer clear of the books shelved in the business or self-help sections, the books with the gleaming covers that shout in forceful red or authoritative blue, with tips on how to manage your time, get promoted, or dress for success, their pages decorated with bullet points, diagrams, and action boxes.

Find the books with paintings or drawings on their covers and on the shelves designated for art or nature, philosophy, theology, spirituality, or literature. No bullet points punctuate their pages, nor do they lend themselves to PowerPoint presentations. Lavish narrative prose creates a seductive lure. In this literature of work, life and humanity are described as they ought be lived and money is nearly a four-letter word.

3. I am drawn to the story of Albert Schweitzer, who at the age of 30, took stock of what he had already received in life. He understood that much in turn would be required of him. So he studied to be a doctor and then headed to Africa, where he was often paid with bananas or eggs. I am drawn to the story of John the Baptist, who lived only on what God gave him: grasshoppers and wild honey.

4. "What do you want to buy someday—a boat?" A financial planner asked my husband and me this question when we were young and newly married, each finally with full-time jobs plus benefits. We both worked for nonprofits. No, we didn't want a boat. I remember her, the planner, dressed in white and sitting in the living room of our rented upper duplex apartment. That apartment had bats in the walls, mice in the cupboards, and a slope to the floor such that a ball dropped under the windows of its west wall would roll out of the bedroom, down the hallway, through the living room, and out on to the porch only to be stopped by its east wall. "A house," we said, "education for our children." With an answer like that, maybe we didn't have the proper materialistic drive to build the kind of portfolio she envisioned. "What else—a vacation home? Travel?" she asked. We stuck with house and education but gave her a check for 100

dollars with the understanding that we weren't in this—this life, this marriage—for the money.

5. Sitting at a table in a café, I asked my husband to think with me about this question and its inevitable permutations. Is money the least or the most significant reason to work? Is a discussion of work a discussion of economics? Does money belong in a discussion about Work with a capital "W"? To my surprise, although I should not have been surprised considering his wrestle with work, my husband gushed about many grand reasons to work, only one of which was related to money. Here are the reasons in the order he gave them: a) to participate in a community and society, and the participation implies that a "need" exists for what one has to give; b) to earn a return on the work, including income; c) to contribute to and help another person; d) to fulfill a God-given purpose; e) to have a place and a reason to apply creativity and passion; f) to have a social position, a place to fit in; g) to hold up your end of things. This perfect listing of reasons to work, to find a job and do it, was his off-the-top-of-the-head intuitive response, and no expert with years of research or pondering can offer better. He mentioned money, but that reason took up about one minute of his 10-minute response. After, there was little left to say. We chewed our pizza, sipped our wine. Through a southwest window, the late-afternoon sun finally reached our table. We've known each other since before our first humble steps into the world of full-time jobs. We know each other's passions and dreams, and we hope one for the other, always. We've awakened to each other's alarms, packed lunches, listened at the dinner table, prayed about meetings, developments, and bosses. We've counted out unemployment checks and celebrated new jobs. He spoke an earned truth.

6. As a teenager, my first job was that of hostess at a dinner theater that ran off-Broadway plays starring actors people knew. I was 15 years old and had to bring the theater manager written permission from my parents and my high school principal. I took the job not to fill a bank account but to buy my first pair of contact lenses.

7. You get a telephone call, and the caller—the employer with whom you interviewed and from whom you have since been hoping to hear—says, "We'd like to offer you a job." Hooray! Then you ask, "How much does the job pay?" Or maybe you don't. Even though this call is with a lowercase "c," it may be linked to the Call that is uppercase—so weighty and grand, you dare not contaminate it by the mention of money.

A STORY

Once I met with a man, upon his request, to help him find a way to make a living by writing. He had tried before, following his bliss by writing the pieces he wanted to write and sending them where no one paid for his work. Finally, he quit writing in order to pay bills. Now, he followed the want ads. His two half-time manual labor jobs, which he didn't like, put some bread on his table but not enough, and he thought there must be another way to make his way with words. He wanted to try again. Articles, newsletters, contracts, clients. What advice can you give me? he asked.

I told him something that I hardly believed I was saying quite so bluntly: "Follow the money." We talked about why. To earn a living someone must buy what he had to sell and at a price that would in turn let him buy heat come winter. Be shrewd as serpents and simple as doves is timeless advice. He didn't hear me. We said our goodbyes. He was like the opposite of the rich young man who wouldn't give up his wealth to save his soul. In his case, he would seek no wealth to save his life.

Reasons to Answer No

1. A check arrived in the mail today. A check for services rendered. I've had one eye on the mailbox and the other eye on my checking account balance and the calendar. Let me list the monthly bills: mortgage plus property tax, gas for heat, electricity, telephone, insurance (home, medical, life, disability), and credit card. Every three months comes the bill from the city for water, sewer, and trash. Every six months is the car insurance and college tuition (multiple). Every quarter, I pay estimated federal and state taxes. Ongoing expenses include groceries, gasoline, clothing, books, prescriptions, giving, deodorant, shampoo, and laundry soap. Clients often pay my invoices late, but I always deliver my services on time. I hesitate before inquiring about the status of any late payment; I don't want to give the appearance that I'm in this just for the money.

2. Josef Pieper might say—and here I'm putting words in his mouth—that work has everything to do with money and so respond to this question with a resounding, "Yes!" Read his writings and you come away with the clear view that work, by definition, is that which is done for a utilitarian purpose, a rally of effort and activity to meet a practical need, such as earning money, or to fulfill a social function. Adam Smith, the founding father of capitalism, would have agreed. Follow this logic, and something done for the sheer passion of it, the inner bliss, the joy in the burst of

creativity and purpose should never be called work, just as a rose should never be called a thorn.

3. I look around my house and see things I wish I had not bought: that magazine, that itchy sweater, that suit with the moth holes that appeared before I even lost the weight to wear it. Perhaps there is a way to go back in time and retrieve every foolish penny spent on a record album, a pair of earrings, concert tickets, tuition, baby car seats, childhood immunizations, half gallons of milk, or bag lunches so as to start again with independent wealth and the freedom it confers to be about a certain kind of work. Or retroactively, create a trust fund from a family whose money was neither old nor new. Or learn to not be afraid to be poor.

4. I see television commercials that go something like this: parents and their young children are playing together on the beach. The father stops to tell the viewing audience that he is so glad they met with financial advisor XYZ before the birth of their first child to set up college and retirement plans so that his children, his wife, and he are ensured of having those needs met. He then returns to dashing in and out of the waves with his family as the camera pans the shoreline but stops before showing the whole truth. The parents in the commercial can and should prudently invest a portion of their earnings every payday, but they can't insure against a stock market "adjustment," corporate reorganization (aka, job loss), medical bills outside the scope of insurance, or any of the other kinks that life can deliver.

5. Perhaps I should have married for money rather than love so as to be free to not concern myself with money, only love. Or learned to live on next to nothing—chopping my wood, milking

cows, bartering for services, and reusing tea bags and coffee grounds. Or finagled a way to inherit a house.

6. The story about my first job continues here. The contact lenses cost 200 dollars, or so I remember. Each time I cashed a paycheck, I put the entire dollar amount in a shoebox and added the change to my five-dollars-every-two-weeks allowance to use as spending money. With the minimum wage then being about two dollars per hour, and work hours limited by school hours, it took awhile to accumulate the needed amount and procure the lenses. Perhaps keeping an eye on the things to be bought is more acceptable than keeping an eye on the money it takes to purchase them, as if that changes the transaction. Buying a house and education may seem more laudable and less materialistic than buying a boat, yet in reality they are significantly more costly. Nothing is free, not even sight.

7. Here is where a position on the stated question can take a final flip before flopping back again or not, swirl uncounted revolutions or portions thereof, and wobble. "Vocation is responsibility and responsibility is a total response of the whole [person] to the whole of reality," wrote Dietrich Bonhoeffer, theologian, pastor, and anti-Nazi conspirator, in his well-known essay on vocation in which he looked at work within the context of multi-dimensional reality. "This life is now my calling," he wrote, and, "responsibility." For Bonhoeffer, the responsibility extended vertically to Christ and horizontally to people and things. Any coordinates along those perpendicular X- and Y-axes are fair game for the would-be uppercase Call. I try to picture this geometry and the infinite number of points in the space between these axes that any life could occupy at any given time. While the vertical, or Y, axis is

indeed outside any system of currency, the horizontal, or X, axis carries a price tag. Yet there is no point for which the horizontal is not paired with the vertical. Isn't there something redemptive in putting food on the table?

THIRTEEN
A Place at the Table

ON MANAGING PINK SLIPS

Sunlight finds its way through the utility window set high in our basement wall and illuminates, just barely, the mahogany-stained oak desk and butcher block worktable, set against adjacent walls, and the space between. Bookshelves and filing cabinets stand in the shadows. This is my office.

Sometimes I walk past its door, see the lamp's glow cast across the desk, and miss sitting there so badly. I glimpse my husband's white coffee cup and long to throw it away and replace it with the cup of my choosing. I see the worktable covered with his stacks and want to clear them off with a single defiant sweep of my arm. I'd pull my chair up to the table and reclaim it. Toss his notes of false leads and plate of leftover lunch. Hang a NO TRESPASSING sign on the door.

To get to my office, you walk down the basement stairs and through the laundry room. Sometimes I used to close my eyes to avoid seeing the laundry piles awaiting my attention. The effectiveness of this act of denial stemmed more from its symbolism than in its true hiding of reality. I knew the piles were there or else I wouldn't have closed my eyes. What's more, the laundry chute from the bedroom hallway empties just to the right of the desk inside the office. Whoosh, whoosh, whoosh; jeans, towels, socks stream down to form a pile of their own that must then be carried into the laundry room. No, closing my eyes simply reminded me that the work I headed for at that moment was not of the laundry variety.

When you walk through the office door, the first piece of furniture you see is the desk. My husband, Dave, found it for me at a yard sale when he was on a morning run in the neighborhood across the creek. He asked the owner to hold it and ran home. "Come back with me and take a look," he said, grabbing his checkbook, so excited because he knew I would love it, and I did. Its top surface area is as big as a door.

Turn to the left and there is the butcher block worktable, made of maple and standing about waist high. Like the desk, its top has the surface area of a door but with the thickness to match. Two-inch-squared pieces of wood are set so that the grain runs horizontally along the length of the table. Glue joints hold the separate pieces tightly together to form a whole. The wood's surface has bleached over time to the color of light straw. Below, its color is darker.

The worktable came from a work venue quite different than the desk. It once stood in the middle of the kitchen in my church's basement. About eight years earlier, someone had the idea to replace it with a 100 percent stainless steel model and demoted the butcher block table to a storage area. Word went out: did anyone want it? Once again, my husband made the discovery and for 25 dollars brought it home for me.

~

Many hands have worked at this table. I think of the women—dead now years—who worked in the kitchen when I was a new and young member of the church: Lilian, Harriet, Doris, Joyce, Irene, Audrey, and Rose. When I inherited this table, it had already served in what was the equivalent of their office for years. On this table they poured Kool-Aid into pitchers and arranged cookies on platters for Sunday school and after-church coffee time. They put cheese in buns, spooned salads into glass bowls for funeral luncheons, and carved ham and rolled meatballs for special dinners.

See the gash at the table's bottom right corner? Maybe someone dropped the silver service teapot while preparing for a bridal shower or the baby shower the women of the church gave me when I was pregnant with my first child. See the slice marks here, there, everywhere? Year after year, the women sliced cardamom bread for the Christmas smorgasbord. They cut sandwiches and rolls in half for the Saturday workdays when a faithful handful of people turned out to wash windows and polish the wooden pews. The scuffs? Perhaps this is where nine-by-thirteen cake pans were slid across the wood.

The worn areas interest me most, the patches where the wood's patina is dull, its grain almost smeared. The women pulled up their stools, sat, and talked, holding cups of freshly brewed coffee, over time their elbows and forearms on the table erasing the joint lines between adjoining pieces. What did they share with each other here in the moments while the food simmered or after drying the last dish?

I like to think the energy of those working hands penetrated the wood of this table. I like to think of the consolations that flowed across its surface.

~

The women of my church used to rotate the job of making the communion bread.

"Do you want a turn?" Lilian asked.

About 70 years old then, Lilian wore glasses, looked a perfect size eight, and styled her dark hair in a classic short curled perm. I remember her always elegant and often in navy blue. Even then—I'm trying to remember—did she have the slight head bob of Parkinson's or did that come only later? I was in my late twenties and without much experience in baking bread, but I liked her and wanted to be part of things.

"Sure," I told her.

Lilian handed me a typed copy of the recipe: "Communion Bread." Her name was at the bottom. The recipe made two loaves. One loaf served the 100 to 150 people typically present on a Sunday morning.

Start with a cup of milk and a stick of butter heated over a gentle flame. Cool slightly. Sprinkle yeast and a touch of sugar into warm water. Whenever I made the bread, I didn't think about how one should approach a sacred task or workspace. Was it sufficient to gather the flour and sugar, yeast and milk, and to scrub the counter? "Let the yeast work a little," wrote Lilian.

Are the milk and butter now lukewarm? Add salt, an egg, more sugar, and the foamy yeast. Stir in some flour, and let this sponge rise. Courting Presence in mere physicalities, even at this early stage before it waited on the altar, suggests the need for prayer and confession as well: *Most merciful God, we confess that we have sinned against you in thought, word, and deed.*

Has the sponge doubled? Stir in more flour; strain against the thickened dough with the spoon until it's impossible to keep on. Overturn the bowl, and drop the dough onto a prepared surface. Knead for 10 minutes with buttered hands. Work the dough thoroughly. Push it down; lift it up. Rotate. Slap it down, fold. Push down again; lift it up. I prepared only by giving my young children—first one child, then two—toys to play with so they would not need me when my hands were coated with butter and flour. "Play is a child's work," my father used to remind me.

Is the dough's surface now smooth with nearly a sheen? When you poke it with a finger, does it bounce back? Place the dough in a covered bowl, and let the yeast work again, doubling the whole. Poke it again: does the impression now remain? Lift the dough from the bowl; divide and shape each half into round flat loaves. Place each in a greased round cake pan. Let the yeast work yet again. Bake the loaves in a hot oven until their color deepens to golden brown. Across their tops, brush melted butter.

A theophany on a mountaintop and Moses came back glowing, but it doesn't always happen like that. This bread may look crusty and brown now, and it will still look crusty and brown held on its paten on the worktable and later in the minister's hands, but don't be fooled, I tell myself. Things aren't always what they seem.

I imagine Lilian and the other women used to make the bread at the worktable in the light from the window above the kitchen sink. I see them assembling mixing bowls, proofing the yeast, and kneading the dough with the push of their hands. On Sunday mornings, they removed the sterling silver paten for the bread and trays for the cups from the locked cupboard. They placed the browned loaf on the paten and poured the Welch's into the clear thimble-like cups, each tucked into its own space in a tray.

At some point, someone figured out the minister more easily broke the loaf—at the moment he holds it up and says, "This is my body broken for you"—if the bottom of the loaf was scored in advance using a sharp knife.

Over the years, I developed a nonbinding unofficial division of labor regarding workspace venue, the last year notwithstanding. The medical writing took place at the desk; the creative writing at the worktable. Sure there were exceptions. Sorting references or making notes on index cards for a medical writing project shifted onto the worktable simply for the surface area needed. Generally, however, the division stood, and so the table's history continued in a new way. What had been a place to prepare food for sustenance or feast, to talk with friends over coffee, and to hold in waiting the quiescent loaf became a place to break life open and gather it up again with words. The words shaped on that table were eager hosts, inviting the Presence to abide with them in a way that words shaped on the desk around comparative percentages and median values could never be.

Shortly before Valentine's Day, nearly a year earlier, Dave lost his job, the fourth time in seven years. I turned my office over to him for his job-search headquarters. I retained use of the filing cabinets, shelves, and drawers, but I gave him the desk and worktable surfaces as well as full, but temporary, occupancy rights.

When Dave and I started dating in our sophomore year of college, he volunteered with the Chicago Mayor's Office for Senior Citizens, helping elderly people keep living in their homes, despite aging-related physical and economic barriers. One afternoon, I went with him to buy groceries for Evelyn, one of his regulars. "Take off all your jewelry before we get there," Dave said. Despite wearing jeans and a white peasant blouse, I looked rich in comparison with the single gold chain around my neck, costume rings, and earrings. We carried the groceries up to her second-floor flat. Someone was bringing her a new mattress later that day, and so we carried the old one downstairs.

For his junior and senior years of college, Dave returned to Minneapolis, his hometown, where he volunteered for Little Brothers of the Poor—Friends of the Elderly. He began to visit Larry and formed a friendship that lasted until Larry died several years later. Larry was about 75 years old with thick white hair and dark-rimmed glasses. He was short and stood simultaneously pitched forward and skewed to one side. He had done time in prison for "playing the numbers" and now lived alone in a red stone apartment building on the poor side of downtown. Larry always wore a sport coat, enjoyed long drags on his cigarettes, and liked to go to nice places for coffee or lunch.

When Larry died, his niece gave Dave a book of poetry Larry had written, typed, and bound with a hard burgundy cover: *Soliloquys* (sic) *About Special Occasions.* In the preface he wrote, "In a colorful career, the author has associated with the best in society, and with the worst, who have drank of the bitter dregs of life, living within the walls of an inner world." Interspersed among the pages are pasted small black and white photographs of the prison yard he called home for awhile. From his poem "Broken Wing":

> The hapless ways of destiny
> Are sometimes cruel with deadly sting,
> To move about mysteriously
> And give a song bird—broken wing.

During one of my trips to Minneapolis to visit Dave, Larry invited us to his apartment so that he and I could meet. Tall stacks of old, yellowed newspapers lined the living room. The sky outside was gray, and little light penetrated the blinds on his living room windows that overlooked the building's parking lot.

Dressed in his traditional sports coat, Larry worked in his narrow kitchen. He boiled water, poured it into three mugs, and added a spoonful of instant coffee to each. He set two Hostess Sno Balls on two plates, one each for Dave and me. He prepared none for himself. Coming back into the living room, he handed us our coffee and treats, then sat down and looked at me as if I were a visiting queen. I lifted the mug for the first sip. A cockroach floated on the coffee's surface.

Larry waited to see the look of pleasure on my face as I drank his brew and ate his store-bought confections. I imagined him walking to a corner store—slowly with a bit of a shuffle, pitched and skewed—and counting out his money.

Looking back now, I probably did a quick calculation figuring that the boiling water sterilized the roach. If it had crawled out from under the Sno Ball, carrying and spreading its compatriot microbes, I likely would have set the plate quietly on the floor untouched. Even at 20, I knew how to calculate risk. Turning my shoulder away from Larry as if looking at something in the far corner of the room, I plucked the roach out and dropped it to the floor. I swung back around and took a sip, "Hmmm...tastes good." I quickly took a bite of the coconut-crusted mound of cake. He smiled, delighted.

What am I doing? I ask myself as I write this. Why even mention the cockroach part of the story? I scold. But then I shrug to myself. Partly, I suppose, because I can't remember this visit without remembering the roach, and I can't remember Larry without this visit, and I can't think of who my husband became and why without remembering Larry. Partly, I suppose, from pride. It pleases me to remember that for a moment I overcame revulsion to cockroaches in order to honor this man's hospitality. That I even remember the roach and mention it now, however, shames me and highlights a difference between Dave and me. If a roach floated in his coffee, Dave would have done the same thing I did—discreetly flicked it out, then proceeded to drink—but he would not mention it later. He would forget about it. So intently did Dave focus on the person who served him the coffee that the signs of poverty all around, which greatly distracted me, for him fell away.

Dave knew what he wanted to do with his life. We used to laugh out loud at its simplicity: he wanted "to help people."

The day we chose my engagement ring—I was by then living in Minneapolis—he picked me up in the Little Brothers' station wagon. He now also worked for them as a driver, transporting their elderly friends to and from appointments, Little Brothers' social gatherings, and other scheduled engagements. I sat in the back seat, and Priscilla, on her way home from a doctor's appointment, rode in the front. She glowed as we let her in on the secret of the engagement and the shopping trip for the diamond.

A graduate degree in gerontology in our first two years of marriage lifted Dave from the position of volunteer and minimum-wage driver to a 20-year career job in human services, one that met his still laughably simple goal. There's nothing laughably simple, however, in navigating life alongside an 85-year-old man who is absolutely alone, with a wife long dead and children who had deleted him from memory years ago; being first to discover a great-grandmother in her recliner the morning after her fatal midnight heart attack; finding the body of a lonely widow decomposing on the floor and churning with maggots; unofficially officiating at funerals and burials, because of the two or three people who showed up to pay their respects, none were a minister or cared to speak; defending in court or in a housing management office a person's right to come home from a post-hospital nursing home stay.

Somewhere in this laughably simple life of helping people, Dave forgot to dress for success, master the latest version of PowerPoint, and eavesdrop on the ivory tower boardroom discussions that prioritized revenue centers over cost centers. While absorbing human burdens for more than 20 years—coming home each evening with their weight heavier and heavier on his shoulders—he didn't take the time to appreciate the magnitude of the shift in standard operating procedure from serving people face-to-face to managing them on paper or to hedge against the trickle-down effects of state and federal budget cuts. The invisible hand of the market and the visible hand of management shook to seal the deal. Such is the prelude to his last seven years of underemployment or unemployment.

We are waiting for the year of jubilee.

~

When I presented the office to Dave, he gratefully moved in. I moved to the dining room table.

Soon stacks of journal articles, books, and working papers lined the dining room walls, surrounded the chair, and extended underneath the table. Sometimes I tripped on a stack when hurrying from my chair into the kitchen to answer the phone, and the papers slid like rocks in an avalanche.

"Please excuse the way the dining room looks. It's my temporary office," I said when guests came over. Out-of-town visitors stayed a week over the summer, and we ate at the table in the kitchen or at a table in the backyard. Friends over for dinner at the start of fall sat in the living room and balanced plates of spaghetti on their laps. In preparation for Thanksgiving, I moved to the desk in my youngest son's room. Two weeks later, however, that son came home from college and needed his room back. I cleared off half a shelf in the hallway closet to store project files, paper clips and pens, CDs, and a blue metal box of receipts. Daily work papers and paraphernalia, I transferred to a cardboard box, white with old mailing labels on the top.

Here are some bills to be paid. Here is an index card containing briefing notes for a conference call this afternoon. Here is my stapler.

Creative writing and household paperwork and work projects all scramble together in the box with no space between. When my son returns to school and the holidays are over, I'll probably plug my laptop in again at his desk or the dining room table. The working office will remain stationed in the box. At least it is mine.

~

Simone Weil wrote about affliction, "In the realm of suffering, affliction is something apart, specific, and irreducible.... It takes possession of the soul and marks it through and through with its own particular mark...." She differentiated affliction from physical pain and suffering, saying the affliction-causing event "that has seized and uprooted a life attacks it, directly or indirectly, in all its parts, social, psychological, and physical." A broken bone can hurt like crazy, but when it's over it's over. Affliction lingers.

Women at the worktable knew affliction. Lilian had Parkinson's disease. Harriet spent years riddled with cancer. Doris suffered from Alzheimer's. Irene buried a daughter who was still a new bride. Other women were rejected by husbands or children.

Some people may think affliction is too strong a word to use for unemployment and underemployment unless it spirals into poverty with the car reclaimed and the house auctioned.

Affliction is not too strong a word.

There are mornings when I am poking through my box, spreading papers across the dining room table, or stealing my son's desk, and I know Dave is lying prostrate—in the tradition of Ezekiel, Ezra, and Daniel—on the basement office floor, on the rectangular space of filtered sunlight, pleading in prayer: let it be over.

The first stage of job loss, sans golden parachute, is panic and fear. Whatever will you do? The second stage: Screw them! You're on to bigger and better. Shake the dust off your feet and move on. The third stage: Business-like determination. Finding a job becomes your job. Start at seven, end at five, and get the job done. Meet the goal. The fourth stage: The unmet goal, instead of resembling a finish line just around the corner, becomes an un-approachable, looming tower that casts a shadow over every inch you travel toward it. Like a mirage, it keeps moving. As much as you believe in yourself or in the one searching for a job, as much as you believe in God to whom you pray for rescue, the smell of failure wafts down and around. You fear others smell it too. That's why they no longer ask, "How's it going?" They stop offering sug-gestions, stop volunteering to make connections or introductions.

You want to wear a sign that lists all the reasons you deserve to report for work, the reasons the guys in the boardroom made a big mistake. You look for a way to hammer your theses to the door of the church. Across the top, the words of Hopkins,

> Thou art indeed just, Lord, if I contend
> With thee; but, sir, so what I plead is just.

Weil wrote that affliction "is a nail whose point is applied at the very center of the soul." A "divine technique," she called it, "a simple and ingenious device." Sounds laughably simple when you put it like that. The same could be said, however, for the invention of a scalpel or a needle. I imagine a doctor bringing a flash of sharp metal close to my skin while saying, "Lie still, this won't hurt a bit," when in fact I know it will hurt a great deal.

To what end, this piercing? I want to ask Weil. A couple paragraphs beyond the image of a butterfly pinned alive into an album she gives an answer, "He whose soul remains ever turned toward God though the nail pierces it finds himself nailed to the very cen-ter of the universe.... this nail has pierced cleanly through all creation, through the thickness of the screen separating the soul from God." If I were to read these words in a strictly academic sense, taking notes as I go, nodding or shaking my head in response according to my agreement or understanding, I would no doubt underline these words and think, *Yes, how provocative, how wise.* Reading them now, however, having seen the flash of metal as my husband was pinned, wings broken, I can only think of its cruelty. It's not yet time for the soliloquy of Joseph—that what his murderous brothers meant for harm, God meant for good.

Meanwhile, my husband and I are in a dance, cheek-to-cheek for a few beats but then flung apart, spinning, only to find each other again for the next measure to repeat the steps. Sometimes our conversations through the laundry-chute, our "intercom" between the main floor and basement office, seem as intimate as holding hands. Other times the space of a floor apart is farther than the distance when he took three buses to get to work. He's humbled and I'm spent—spent by the boiling over of my work needed to sustain income, spent carrying my box, spent by my own pinning to the dining room table.

Lilian once told me when she was a young wife, she used to lie on her dining room table while her husband put all kinds of trial contact lenses in her eyes. Her husband was an optometrist and a significant player in the development of contact lenses back in the 1930s and 1940s.

I wonder what she thought, lying there on her back as her husband's finger approached with the glint of glass or plastic and placed one experimental disc after another on her eyeball. Her husband, no doubt, hoped to help people see and recruited her in that pursuit. Did she thrill to be part of the experiment or did she grumble, lying on the table again and again while rice boiled over on the stove or her children demanded attention? When one lens after another wasn't quite right, did she smell failure? Surely she wanted the uncertainty to be over and her dining room table returned to its rightful function.

Lilian's physical sacrifice impresses me. At the age of 16, I got my first pair of contact lenses, made from the same hard Lucite material for which she had been a guinea pig. The contact lens specialist laid the blue-tinted discs on a white towel. He showed me how to put a drop of wetting solution onto the disc's concave surface, balance it on one finger, hold the eye open wide with another finger, then move the finger with the lens toward the eyeball until contact. The trick was not to flinch. An eye clenched shut can't accept the lens. I followed his lead and achieved two Lucite-covered eyes. A pinch of sand in each may have been more comfortable.

Tears poured—*flush this intruder out!* To hold my eyes open required steel resolve; I braced to simply blink. Only the prospect of a face free from glasses kept me from pulling at the corner of my eyes to release the lenses and waving good-bye as I walked out the door. One hour in the eyes the first day, two hours the next, and so on, as advised. I progressively acclimatized my eyes to reach a full day of wear and left the glasses at home in a drawer.

How did Lilian keep the unperfected trial lenses in her eyes *and* hold her eyes open sufficiently for her husband to take measurements and assess comfort? I imagine her in pain, tears streaming as she allowed her husband to do his work, his experimenting, hardly able to keep her eyes open, but somehow she did.

Prisoners are poets; bread and words become Presence; tears yield to sight.

Life isn't what it seems. I know this. Yet, sometimes, I wish I had a fitted disc of Lucite to place over the whole thing in order to see it for what it really is.

Seven years before my first contact lenses, I got my first pair of glasses, tortoise-shell cat-eye frames. Wearing them for the first time, sitting in the front passenger seat of the rust-colored Ford station wagon as my mother drove home, I was stunned to see that the leaves on the trees we zipped past were separate entities. The trees were not undifferentiated masses of green like in a pre-schooler's drawing. Of course, I knew this about foliage, but the sharper reality that opened the moment I watched thousands and thousands of individually bordered green wedges, scallops, and slivers waving from tree trunks dazzled me. I remember the shift from seeing through a glass darkly to now face-to-face. To think this had been there to see all along—I couldn't stop looking.

With my first contact lenses, that kind of clarity was present any which way I turned my head or rolled my eyes, straight ahead or out of peripheral vision. My field of vision raced beyond what I imagined possible. A price had been paid, however, which the glasses had not exacted. Clarity with the lens came only after my eyes adjusted to the presence of what they didn't want. The tearing had to pass before I could see.

My husband would like nothing better than to remove his coffee cup from my desk, discard his stacks—kick them even, kick them hard—rip to shreds all his job search notes, and come to me at my cardboard box and lead me by the arm down the stairs and back into my office. The lamp's glow and morning sunlight through the window would welcome me. There now, he'd say, life is normal again; we've reached the algorithm's end. He kisses me goodbye, puts on his coat, picks up his briefcase, and heads out to the start of his new full-time job with benefits. He waves as he backs the car out of the driveway. I remove the stapler from my box, along with the notes for the conference call, sigh with relief at the homecoming, and get to work.

For now, however, my sigh is one of resignation. Or maybe it's a sigh to draw attention to how hard I'm working. Or perhaps the sigh is more like "see me be brave," like plucking a roach from my drink. Could I ever just drink the cup, roach and all?

There are so many kinds of work: the work of earning a living, creating, serving; the work of looking for work. The work of marriage. Raising children. The work of the yeast, the work of the spirit. The work of play. The work of the church. Laundry. The preparing of food.

What should we call the work happening inside of us? George MacDonald used words like *burning*, *whirl*, and *reel*.

> But thou art making me, I thank thee, sire.
> What thou hast done and doest thou know'st well,
> And I will help thee: gently in thy fire
> I will lie burning; on thy potter's-wheel
> I will whirl patient, though my brain should reel.

Weil calls affliction a technique. That implies work too. Is affliction a work of God? I need that disc of Lucite to see clearly; the joint between His work and mine blurs.

~

Life isn't what it seems. I know this, but also don't.

What if my husband and I played along anyway?

We could take each stack off the worktable, one by one. Remove the file folders. The cup of pens, the pile of paper clips. The box of note cards, the bills. The lamp. I'd hold a clean white cloth under hot water, wring it out, and sweep it back and forth across the wood's surface, wiping away dust and paper fibers and drops of spilled coffee.

We could bring something new to the table.

Here now is the warm milk and melted butter. The yeast with its sugar, swirling in water, foaming and lifting. Let it work a little, reminds Lilian. Here is the flour ready to be transformed.

The whole sticky mess: push it down, lift it up. Rotate. Slap down, fold. Push it down again, lift it up. The parts of the whole become one. The stubborn flesh now lets the impression remain. Bake in a hot oven until it sounds hollow when tapped.

We could place the steaming bread on a plate of our best china—white, glazed gray, circled in blue—and set it on the rescrubbed worktable between two burning white candles.

Here is the wine, like a garnet, in its chalice.

We'd each pull up a stool. Sit close, shoulders touching, our forearms on the spots where the wood's finish has been worn by years of forearms not our own. The reflection of the flames luminates the presence of one for the other and dances off the evidence of job dead ends now scattered on the floor.

Take and eat. Pre-broken, we'd tear hunks of bread from the loaf. *Drink.* For our thirst, we'd gulp.

ACT III

Where we encounter love, devotion, and guidance; the sacrament of the present moment and every moment; a never-ending journey; prayer, grace, and surrender; strength; two views of time; patience and transformation; and a blessing of countenance.

O God, that at all times you may find me as you desire me and where you would have me be, that you may lay hold on me fully, both by the Within and the Without of myself, grant that I may never break this double thread of my life.

—Pierre Teilhard de Chardin, *The Divine Milieu*

FOURTEEN
Spinning and Being Spun

ON WHERE GUIDANCE COMES FROM

To leave on a trip is a kind of dying. In fact it may be the closest to death a person can come while still alive and well. The plans for all I will finish before walking out the front door and boarding the plane are sweeping; it is not enough that I pack my suitcase. I habitually regard these moments of leaving as due dates by which time my life will be in order, a goal that is, of course, never met. The life that must be ordered rolls forward quickly in those pre-travel days, and the minute arrives after which nothing more can be done.

More minutes please.

No, the minutes granted must be enough, whether or not they are.

I sit in seat 18C on a morning flight from Minneapolis to Albuquerque. From there I'll take a shuttle van to Santa Fe, this journey's final destination. Ten days away from paid work and at a different kind of work, a graduate school residency, an interlude and expense any financial planner would tell us we can ill afford.

My luggage is stowed away in the plane's cargo hold. The packed clothes were washed: one check mark off my pre-travel to-do list. I sewed three buttons on two blouses and repaired a dropped hem: three more check marks. I bought toothpaste, dental floss, granola bars, and almonds.

"Just under the wire before I leave, here is the first draft manuscript," I wrote in an email to a client late the night before. "Now to finish packing," I sign off.

I printed out two copies of my itinerary and placed one in my purse and the other on the kitchen table. I asked my husband to water the geranium by the back door and the impatiens by the front door. I kissed him good-bye and hugged my sons.

Crumbs are on the kitchen floor, however. Stacks of papers cover the dining room table and the floor around it. The refrigerator shelters unpleasant developments in clear plastic containers with blue lids. My underwear drawer is a mess. Three baskets of laundry hold unfolded clothes and unmatched socks. At least 10 people didn't receive their expected email or returned telephone call. My youngest son is two days out of a second wrist surgery with eight days left to go on antibiotics and until his follow-up visit with the surgeon, when we learn whether the surgery worked. My oldest son will move out to start his real adult life before I return. There are invoices I have not mailed; receipts not recorded; prayers not prayed; groceries not purchased. An idea for a book is scribbled somewhere and buried at the same depth as notes about alternate careers I maybe should have pursued or might yet someday.

What comprises the life ready for death? Surely crumbs and unmatched socks are not mortal sins of commission or omission and would not be held against me if this plane went down. Neglect of sons or husband would not be so equivocal. But what of a dis-regarded career interest or the seed of a creative project abandoned without water or light? On one of those points will God note a hole in the universe, however tiny, and thereafter regard me with a tone of disappointment? Have I done the work I was made for? I wonder these things even as I pray for divine guidance, even as I believe in guidance, even as I fear a misread or withheld sign.

A friend of mine died in 10 weeks time. I often think of her in these moments of departure. An aggressive cancer ravaged her body, and a hospital bed was moved into her living room before she even had time to put away the laundry or straighten her dress-er. Time was called and that was that: turn your paper over and put your pencil down. A couple weeks before she died, I spent an af-ternoon helping at her house. Signs of her works-in-progress—a grocery list, stacks of paperwork, a basket of unfolded clothes, framed photographs of three daughters—lay halted on tabletops and the floor like a display of artifacts from Pompeii.

At her funeral, her memorial card bore a verse she chose from Micah, "And what does the Lord require of you? To act justly and to love mercy and to walk humbly with your God." I know this is the bottom line, the question worth the most points on the final vocational exam, yet the corollary questions remain: how, when, and where? The acting and loving and walking can't be in the ab-stract, but must be anchored in time and place—moving arms and legs, fingertips and brain. And hopefully a paycheck is earned in the process.

There are moments that are like lines in the sand. The storage bins latch; the external doors close. "At this time, please turn off all cellular appliances, including cell phones." The plane backs away from the gate and taxis along the asphalt labyrinth that leads to the runway. There is nothing more to be done.

It is finished.

Twice before I've been to Santa Fe, the land that points to the sky. About Santa Fe, Willa Cather wrote, "Elsewhere the sky is the roof of the world; but here the earth was the floor of the sky. The landscape one longed for when one was far away, the thing all about one, the world one actually lived in, was the sky, the sky!" On my first visit under this infinite vault, I made my way to the center of town where artists display their handcrafted jewelry: the Native Americans with their goods spread on blankets beneath the portal of the Palace of the Governors; the artists who lack such a pedigree with theirs on tables along the perimeter of the center Plaza. I wanted turquoise earrings and found a pair that was exactly right at one of the Plaza tables. Dangling, polished turquoise cut to ovals the size of grapes, with the right combination of iron and copper to make them not too blue and not too green, and encircled by a sterling silver band. Turquoise, I've read, is the color of yearning.

When I returned to Santa Fe the following summer, I had in my mind to get a ring to match the earrings. Back to the Plaza and to the middle of the square's east side, back to the same table from the year before and the same artist. She wore a gray tank top and her long, dark blonde hair lay kinked and matted down her neck and shoulders, her skin leathered from the sun.

"I bought these earrings from you last year," I said, pointing to the turquoise ovals that hung from my ears. "Do you have a ring to match?" I expected a smile, her gratified acceptance of my implicit compliment, her eagerness to please me, the customer.

"I don't do rings. Never have," she said, her face an unmoving matrix of self-knowledge and mission. Without even a sympathetic pause, she turned away. Three words in red lettering stared at me from the back of her shirt:

> smart
> strong
> bold

I returned her dismissal with envy. Oh to be so clear on what you do and what you don't do, so unmoved by flattery or suggestion, so untempted by money ready to be placed in your hand.

A Vocation Primer, Part 1

God to Adam

> *By the sweat of your brow you will eat your food.*

God to Moses

> *What is in your hand?*

Moses to God

> *Establish thou the work of our hands.*

Mordecai to Queen Esther

> *Who knows but you have been placed here for such a time as this?*

Samuel to Saul

> *Once these signs have been fulfilled, whatever your hands find to do, do it.*

Aristotle

> *Work to live.*

Mary

> *Let it be to me as you have said.*

Jesus

> *If it be thy will, let this cup pass from me.*

Michelangelo

> *Painting is not my trade!*

Simone Weil

> *. . .obedience. . . .*

Georgia O'Keefe

> *One paints what is around.*

∼

I always watch when a flight attendant gives the safety demonstration: click and tighten your seat belt; place your own oxygen mask first; the seat is a flotation device. We all know these things and don't need to watch. Few do. Gripping tickets freely and willfully purchased, most, if not all, the passengers have buckled themselves in unaided and don't care that the attendant prepares us to take turns no one either expects or would choose to take. Like the Philosophy 101 question about the tree that falls that no one hears, if no one looks up from their magazines will the attendant's action have meaning? Must offered work also be received? I wonder these things, and so in flight after flight keep my eyes on hands pointing out nearest restrooms and call buttons.

Seated in 18C, I watch the recitation this flight's designated attendant gives. He's a middle-aged man, balding with a slight comb-over hairstyle. His white shirt appears worn and a bit yellowed. His pants are pleated and belted under a slight paunch. He seems a bit rattled, lacking that all-is-in-control veneer of the typical flight attendant.

I can't be sure of course, but I suspect he was called at the last minute to report for duty, to fill in for a sick crew member. I imagine his phone rang and awakened him on his day off. He groggily said yes to the call, "Can you come?" His wife got out of bed and made him coffee. He pulled the shirt out of the dirty clothes hamper and tried to shake out the wrinkles. He held it up under the light, looking for overt stains that might give away his laundering shortcut. Later today, if he'd had the day off, he'd planned to get a hair cut, planned to sign up at his local gym, planned to take his wife out for dinner, planned all sorts of things. But here he is, back at work for another day of pay and doing his job well but for the portion of himself he is holding in reserve, as if by holding something back, he can get his personal day after all, as if he can have his job and life too.

His arms pivot toward the exit doors as he reminds us, "The nearest exit may be behind you." On this day of his frazzle, maybe one set of eyes on him as he clicks the seat belt buckle for the three thousandth time will be sufficient reward that he picked up his phone and said, "yes."

"Flight attendants, prepare for takeoff," says the pilot over the PA. All seats are in an upright position. The nose of the plane turns toward the runway, and the engines fire. Rows and rows of passengers face forward; the steady acceleration pushes our backs against our seats, and in unison we tilt back and are carried upward into the sky.

That summer day on my second time in Santa Fe, I found and bought a turquoise ring elsewhere. Leaving the artist who doesn't make rings, I crossed the street to the Palace of the Governors. Blue, green, and burgundy blankets lay side by side in a row the length of a city block as if ready for a picnic if the goods don't sell. On the blankets were pendants, necklaces, earrings, rings, guitar picks, barrettes, and brooches made of silver, copper, turquoise, coral, and lapis. Each Native American artist or artist's representative presided over his or her wares from the head of the blanket, seated either on a chair, a low stool, or the veranda floor.

Small crowds gather at each blanket, and so patrons often wait for a turn to look down, crouch, pick up, and try on. I saw a ring but couldn't reach it. The young woman with long black hair, seated on a stool, smiled and reached out with a long narrow stick she kept on the floor next to her. She slid one end of the stick through the ring's opening, lifted it from its black velvet display box, and glided it dangling from the stick to my hand. I slid the ring on my finger.

"Did you make this?" I asked.

"Yes," the woman said, and she showed me where the band bore her maker's mark.

It was a split ring, open in the middle, for design purposes of course, but also conveniently accommodating the changing ring size of women throughout a lifetime or the month, like elastic in a pair of durable pants. On one side of the split is an oval turquoise, more blue than the earrings and with fewer veins. Along the stone's perimeter, a hefty sterling silver band curves ever so slightly over its surface as if the stone were floating on hidden water and would bounce right up without the metal's angled hold.

The other side of the split is a vertical silver bar. Engraved in the silver bar and around the band is a zigzag design—a mountain range, the woman told me. It means journey.

Sometimes it's hard to keep your eyes off the fiercely progressive right tail of a bell-shaped curve. The man across the aisle in 18D bows his head with such intensity toward his laptop, screen glowing, and toward his papers, marked with yellow highlighting and scribbles of black ink, that I could be easily convinced he answers a jealous and demanding call: cure cancer, erase the national deficit, put a man on Mars, satisfy hunger on any and every level. There's a woman just like him seated right behind. And the man next to her. Later, jolting down the aisle toward the restroom, I see open books, their covers glossy, many adorned with a famous portrait, a queen or a general, an adventurer or a painter, at this seat and the next a biography of a heroic man or woman who saved a civilization or a city block or a child or the soul of a people. Surrounded by all this heroism and destiny, I start to wonder if the rest of us—mingled together in the bell's dome, in the vicinity of the mean or median or any other word for ordinary—should have listened harder to the still small voice calling in the night or were just a bit too hasty when signing up for an unremarkable life.

I have two vocations, no three, maybe four; or is one—or two?—of them just a job—or a career?—and the rest vocations? Or maybe one is a call, and the rest are vocations. Or roles? Who knows how many of what I have. I grow weary of trying to sort them, rank them, judge them; negotiate their spats; document their origins; appease the one or two temporarily neglected;

humble the one or two attended. I walk over and around multiple mountains; I don't aim for a single peak. The writings of some experts who claim to know about these things tell me that I have failed, with my life's single purpose—some call it one's cross, others call it one's bliss—undiscovered and unclaimed. The writings of other experts tell me this is the way of a pilgrim. I know I am tired much of the time.

When I arrive at my destination, I will call my husband for news of his latest job interview. Déjà vu and he is in another round of unemployment. So here I am again in another season of super-employment, giving long hours to work that is at once a gift and a curse. I am also one year into a graduate program, a yes to a whisper, an obedient step, playing my hand. Like a trapeze artist who lets go of one support before grabbing hold of the next, I had hoped to do this without the pressure or time-constraints of earning a full-time income. Instead, I dangle suspended between the chosen life and the given life, sometimes losing track of which is which. I think about the flight attendant with the yellowed shirt who looks like he's supposed to be someplace else and see me in him.

During the first week of college, I took a career aptitude test to learn what I'd be good at, or at least, what I might like being. A series of preference questions (*Which of the following would you rather do?*) claims to translate the mystery formed in the womb into an alpha-numeric code of blackened A, B, C, and Ds for questions numbered one and beyond, like a knitting pattern that could never describe how the finished cashmere scarf will wrap around your neck just so, cradling and warming and soothing, and last for a hundred years, or catch on a nail tomorrow and unravel, or give you a rash out of the blue.

I can't be sure about this either, but I suspect that when the flight attendant took the career aptitude test his freshman year of college, his current career was not among those recommended to him. About my age, he seems an unlikely candidate for the job title "stewardess" in the mid-1970s. I would bet this is not his first career, but a person has to choose a place to start. Even no decision is a decision, my father used to tell me. You plant your flag somewhere and begin. But where you start, where you end up, and where you go in between are all very different places. Or so it would seem. If I remember correctly, two of the careers the test findings suggested for me were lawyer and librarian, neither of which I became, although it is not lost on me that in my work I daily sort through online holdings of the National Library of Medicine to find relevant evidence for claims made, and even now on this page, here I am testing truth, or at least looking for it, with words.

If any of us on this Airbus 320 get cold or tired while flying southwest through the sky, all we have to do is push the call button located above our seat next to the light, and the flight attendant will come. "How can I help you?" he'll ask. Then nodding he'll say, "Of course," and hurry away, only to return with a blanket and a pillow. If the oxygen masks were ever to come down, he would be one of the few to keep his head on his shoulders. If he had been born in another time and place, he would be the one risking his life to guide the pulling up of the draw bridge to the walled city as the invaders approached. He would be giving juice and sandwiches to the tired and weary at Ellis Island or announcing air raid instructions in London during World War II. His eye may have been on roles with kings or presidents or boards of directors, but his hand would be offering something to someone, or his firm voice showing them the way.

There are moments that are like lines in the sand. Human agency and circumstance—whether divine will or chance or some Job-like backstory—crash or embrace along the line's infinite points. Here is the mystery of what becomes of us. Here is where five-year plans morph like holograms, and arms trained to sculpt are twisted to paint frescoes. Here is where the cup is lifted; the head bows in the active passivity of *let it be*; the hands dig and pick, hoping for the right blend of metal and mineral to reflect the ethereal vault in stone.

"There is no need to bother about what has been told to others; there are words for you alone," wrote Jean-Pierre de Caussade, a Jesuit priest born in Toulouse, France in 1675. Ever since reading *The Sacrament of the Present Moment,* de Caussade's collected talks and letters to the nuns in Nancy, France, it has been the Gordian knot in my brain. Divine action shapes every moment, suggests the priest. I want to say in response that reasonable people could argue the origin of any moment; who can know? It doesn't matter, de Caussade would say, because all you can do is respond. Our task is to do our duty to God according to Scripture and submit to the present moment by responding according to felt impulse, which should be shaped by the divine if we are being faithful to the aforementioned duty. Trust the felt impulse at every step: to pick up the phone, or not; to say yes, or not; to get up and go, or not; to discern the authority behind the call and yield to it the authority in the soul, or not.

His thesis sounds well and good, but I remind myself that it is never this easy. One thousand and one impulses to do this and do that flood my mind everyday. Which are of God? Which are of me? Likewise, every task, obstacle, and burden carries choices at every turn. Like the Amazing Labyrinth game my children used to play, which path to take at any given moment is the looming question, answered without foresight, but gut or reason or fear or peace or any other inner guides for action or inaction. "All we need to know is how to recognize his will in the present moment," wrote de Caussade. Ah, there's the rub! My current impulse may or may not equal God's will, to which de Caussade would object by challenging my degree of self-surrender, trust, and faith, or the degree to which I've accomplished the aforementioned prerequisite duty. This challenge I must sustain.

I look back and could fall on my knees right here and now in gratitude for the currents that seemed to carry me—yes, this is the man; yes, this is the house; yes, this is the job ad to answer, the number to write down, the time to make the call; no, look away, pass by. A book jumps off the shelf in front of my eyes, and I know it is for me and life is never the same. The moment at hand brings an impulse of joy or action or warning, and I am all for de Caussade's sacrament nomenclature. Yes, yes, yes; come, present moment, come—God with us. But darken the moment with tragedy or disappointment or even the shadow of cons across the pros, and my impulse is to not trust in divine impulse, to reject the moment.

To paraphrase de Caussade: calm, calm; there is a hiding place where silk is spun in secret. "Everything leads to union with him; everything brings about perfection excepting sin and what is not our duty," wrote de Caussade. "Only take things as they come without interfering. Everything guides, purifies and sustains you, carrying you along, so to speak, under God's banner by whose hand earth, air and water are made divine."

I believe; help my unbelief.

~

A VOCATION PRIMER, PART 2

There is a scene in Ingmar Bergman's *Fanny and Alexander* that is worth the whole film to me. It is Christmas Eve and the Ekdahl family's theater group has just given a performance of the nativity story. The patriarchal son gathers together his maids and servants, their arms laden with baskets of gifts and the filled silver platters and bowls of a feast. He reminds them to be gracious to the theater staff, "a mixed lot," and then lifts a flaming silver bowl and leads the parade down the stairs to the theater stage. Everyone sings and those with free hands clap. Musicians on strings and horns accompany them as they sashay around the spent performers before finally placing the beverages, food, and gifts on the candle-studded serving table. "Help yourselves, everybody," says the son. "Step forward; don't be shy."

In the next frame, the theater manager, another of the Ekdahl sons and an actor in the group, steps up on a small platform. His face is flushed and exhausted. The feast—consumed or waiting, we can't be sure—edges his peripheral vision as he looks into the faces of the 30 or 40 members of the theater staff gathered around him. He played the part of Joseph and only now removes his wig. He looks to be about 55 years old. He tells us that he has stepped up on this platform as the theater manager for 22 years, "without really having any talent." He laughs; they laugh. He removes the fake mustache and then the beard. His hair is plastered to his head from sweat.

"My only talent," he continues, "is that I love this little world." His eyes are bordered by lines and deep circles. He looks down more than up. His eyes glisten. He hesitates and swallows hard and talks again. He sighs with a quiver, trying not to cry, like a new mother exhausted from labor, like a creator letting go of his created. His audience is silent. All eyes meet his. No one rustles; no one moves; no ones flips the pages of a magazine. Like a hen, he would gather his chicks and the whole barnyard under his wings if he could. God's presence expanded yet again from temple to person and now to this theater with its tired huddled mass.

I want to freeze that frame and study that face of love. I want to magnify every pixel and look for evidence of causation. Which came first: the job or the vocation? The chosen or the given, the creator or the created, the moment or the response, the call or the love? I want to unlock Oscar Ekdahl from the film, escort him down from the platform, and ask him to teach me.

Do I give away too much if I tell now that this man dies before many more scenes have played out? Do I give away too much if I tell I envy the catch in his throat?

Midway through the flight to Albuquerque and somewhere over Nebraska, the man in seat 18B and I start talking. Seated, he looms more than a head above me, a large man, not in weight but in frame. He wears glasses, has thinning white hair, and is dressed in khakis and a sport shirt. He tells me he is in his eighties. I note his tight and vibrant skin and conclude he is active and well. As we talk, we reach for pouches of trail mix and cans of Sierra Mist on the pull-down trays in front of us.

"Are you from Minneapolis?" I ask.

"No, just changed planes there this morning," he replies.

"Is Albuquerque your final destination?"

"Yes, I'm going to see my daughter."

"A vacation?"

"No, she's in the hospital, dying."

He tells me that his daughter's cancer has spread. They will be saying their good-byes. He tells me how his wife also died of cancer at the same age his daughter is now. He tells me another daughter is only a year behind this one in age. "Of course she is afraid," he says. I ask the dying daughter's name, and say I will pray for her—and him.

We then munch and sip and talk of things other than death. The plane is at its cruising altitude, above all possibility of clouds and where the sky is perpetually clear, robin-egg blue in the daytime, coal black in the night. Now, just past noon, the sun shines brightly through the airplane windows, so brightly that some people in surrounding rows have lowered the shades. The man tells me that he looks forward to getting on the plane at the end of it all and going back home, back to his fishing boat.

Our legs are in need of a stretch and our backs long to lengthen and stand. His arms fidget, and I bend my neck this way and that to relieve a kink. The flight attendant comes by and clears our wrappers and napkins, our empty aluminum cans, our plastic cups holding the dregs of melted ice. He'll come by again later, holding a full tray, and offer us water.

FIFTEEN
Summa Laborum III

ON WHO GETS CALLED
AND FOR WHAT (A DEBATE)

THE QUESTION

Do only some people, doing certain kinds of work, have a call
or vocation?

REASONS TO ANSWER YES

1. It seems that there are words and definitions with inclusion and
exclusion criteria, and that how you slice and dice it all to answer
the question at hand depends on the part of history with which
you choose to align. Antiquity: when the leisure to contemplate
the spiritual side of any endeavor, and thereby pursue a call or
vocation, was accessible only to the free man who did not labor.
The Middle Ages: when the church held that only priests and
nuns had vocations. The early Reformation: when Luther taught
that a person's current occupation, lived in response to God, was

a vocation. The later Reformation: when Calvin spoke in stronger terms and taught that God calls some people to stay in their current occupation and others to move to something new, but all should work to transform the world. The 1600s: when the Puritans advanced Calvin's teachings and emphasized God's call to work for the common good. The early 1900s: when Weber claimed that vocation and capitalism went hand in hand. Now: when a contingent believes that people have calls or vocations only if they are in a position to reform the world; another contingent requires that one's giftedness or charisms be employed; another contingent holds that the concept of vocation should be unlocked from work and more appropriately paired to life as a whole; another contingent preaches self-fulfillment; another contingent simply has an internal drive to give a job or career their all.

2. Vocation derives from the Latin *vocare*, meaning call, meaning a caller has called, meaning a phone is ringing, and maybe it's for you or maybe not, because the calls always seem to come to others who played their cards right. So you wait and hope, straining to hear your name. Or so it feels sometimes.

3. Look around, and you'll find the preponderance of contemporary expert opinion on the side of a one-to-one correlation between call and the only work worth doing. The system that links the two is the Holy Grail. An email just arrived advertising a continuing education opportunity from a local seminary. The advertised workshop uses a trademarked process to help you discern what God is calling you to be.

4. Vocations are found. They are discerned or discovered, implying they elude and baffle, unearthing themselves only for those who learn the secret or stumble into the hidden cache.

5. Gatekeepers have established themselves and written standards by which workers can assess the vocation-worthiness of the work they do, thereby knowing what group they will be in when the goats are separated from the sheep. Buechner famously ruled out writing television commercials for deodorant and jobs with which the worker is bored.

6. Can you answer "yes" to the following questions: Is the work just? Is it a fit for your gifts? Is it artful or craftsmanlike? Is it independent? Does it feel like play? Is it true, good, and beautiful? Is it self-fulfilling?

7. And this: Is there a direct correlation between your personal mark on a product or outcome and your breath in a prayer?

∾

A Story

Together with a host of other parents and gowned graduating sons and daughters, I sat in the arena bleachers, looking down at the assembly of students and faculty in the space where basketball players regularly dribbled and passed, and listened to the Liturgy of the Word. The Gospel reading was from John 15. We stood while the priest read. At this college baccalaureate service, there had been no picking and choosing an appropriate passage, like one on a Hallmark card, one with the right message for the occasion, such as: I will give you success; I will give you your heart's desire; all things are possible; go and conquer. The prescheduled, predetermined lectionary—observed worldwide—dictated verses 9 through 17 from that chapter of John as the reading for that week in that liturgical year, conforming the occasion to the Word rather than the other way around.

The priest read words of love spoken by Jesus. "Remain in my love," he read. "Love one another, as I love you," he read. "No one has greater love than this, to lay down one's life for one's friends." In his homily he then spoke of love. Agape. Phileo. Eros. "But turn your attention to agape," he said. This is the sacrificial kind of love, the laying down of one's life for another. You high-achieving graduates, aspire to this, he said, not to success.

The young men and women in his audience would go forth to be temps, employees, contractors, and business owners in all manner of workplaces: cafés and schools, hospitals and banks, courts and hardware stores, museums and malls, libraries and factories, nursing homes, publishing companies, grocery stores, advertising agencies. At the service's end, he blessed them one and all.

Reasons to Answer No

1. Beyond words and definitions, language has moods. The indicative mood states things in black and white: *You do*, or *You do not*. The interrogative mood makes a request: *May I?* The imperative mood asserts agency within the context of an other: *Give me*. The subjunctive mood carries the sense of possibility as the speaker's utterance spins from the here and now out into the future or back into the past and begins to lay bare a heart set on something: *I could do*, or *I would have liked*. The optative mood fans the flame of the subjunctive's longing: *Oh that I could* or *Would that it were so*. Consider the famous assent of Mary: "Let it be to me as you have said." I'm not enough of a grammarian to know exactly which mood fits this sentence, but it suggests to me the

intersection of optative and imperative: not only a longing to receive but also a choosing to receive.

2. Vocation derives from the Latin *vocare*, meaning call, but also summons, which goes a step further than call. A summons is a call into existence, meaning resuscitation and breath, humanity and personhood; meaning your name has indeed been spoken, has been called; meaning the only question on the table is whether you'll call back ever and always, even through your work.

3. Here are my questions: Has any call, vocation, or gifted-ness assessment tool—with inventories and worksheets evaluating personal preferences, even those that are trademarked or stamped with some version of a governing body's stamp of approval—ever been validated against the intention of God, the supposed caller? Has any assessment tool ever demonstrated a perpetual monitor-ing feature so as to detect an out-of-the-blue shift, such as when Samuel heard his name spoken in the night and answered "Here I am" or when Jesus told the fishermen to leave their nets?

4. Take out a clean piece of paper and write the words "vo-cation" and "call," but leave room on the page for an expanded lexicon. Add the word "subject," a word that poet and essayist Fanny Howe uses repeatedly in her memoir of vocation. It's the big question you're always trying to answer, the meta-problem you're always trying to solve; who doesn't have one of those? And with what situation can't that subject be juxtaposed? I'm picturing our lives as subjects like books, a living Dewey Decimal system, and God, at the time of our birth or at a moment when the scene opens for such a time as this when all things work together, say-ing, "Now." For this subject it is time, and we open. Write the words "inscape" and "instress," and credit them to Gerard Manley

Hopkins: inscape, the essence of a person that pulls the personality together as if by a vortex before spinning a force, instress, back out into the world as action of the mind or will. Write the word "Spirit," juxtapose it with inscape and instress, and you have something completely new.

5. The alarm clock will go off tomorrow morning as it does every morning, and the whole reason to get out of bed is at stake. I am Everyman—*Imago Dei*—and I want to know that my hand is slapping the alarm and throwing back the covers to engage in something bigger than myself. I want to know that in the eight hours or more that is a work day, while my hands and my brain are doing what they are consigned to do by the requirements of my job, they are simultaneously sweeping through other layers of meaning as if life was the sacred text that it is.

6. How many hoops must a worker jump through before he trips and counts himself out of the game?

7. Sitting facing the south window, I'm praying, my work in stacks around me. The afternoon sun lights the back of my closed eyelids, red burnished with gold and flecks of green. Church bells ring. Clouds cover the sun, and the membranous ocular screen now glows purple. A dog barks three times. My hands are cupped, one inside the other, on my lap, asking, longing to receive. Imperative and optative harmonize. *Establish Thou the work of my hands,* from the psalm of Moses, moving in and out with my breath.

SIXTEEN
One Thousand and One Tales of Now

ON TIMING

An alarm clock sounds; a work call begins; a project is due; the water bill is due. The time is *chronos,* meaning ordinary time, time that marches, time that drags or races. Yet grander stories are being spun all the time, coursing through the current right above our heads, just out of reach for now. Threads of this twist with threads of that, transfiguring the whole, out of sight. The time is *kairos,* meaning the right time, time in between like a bridge (think: *metaxu),* time that gathers toward fullness, time that breaks like the sun through parted clouds.

I once traveled to a medical conference in the city of the Golden Gate Bridge and Ghirardelli chocolate and stayed at a hotel that identified itself with Aladdin's genie, or so it would seem. Their guests' wishes were their commands. "Whatever you want. Whenever you want it," was their mission. They coaxed us to take them up on the claim by suggesting ideas: How about a bathtub filled with champagne and strawberries? Or a pet goldfish to keep you company during your stay? Perhaps a wedding—pronto? Or a spur-of-the-moment mariachi band? "What is your wish?" they asked. "We'll fulfill it," they promised.

It's tempting to forget about *kairos* given the clamor of *chronos*.

The hotel lobby was dark when I walked in. The clouds outside guaranteed it. Lit only by the daylight filtered through the front revolving doors and the candles along the front desk and opposite counter, darkness must prevail there on even the sunniest days. Acoustic music with an Eastern ring played in the background, giving the place the feel of an upscale cross between a late-1970s disco and the genre of 1960s gift shop that sold incense and psychedelic posters.

Strands of silver beads hung from ceiling to floor behind the front desk. Blue lights flashed beneath the strands. From a projector across the room, words traveled to spill out across the beads:

> Wish. Command.
> Whatever/Whenever.

Hotel guests arriving for the conference were more interested in studying and healing diseased livers than bathing in champagne. Most of these guests were doctors. Long before they would be told by the genie hotel that their wishes might be commands, each had already wished to be what they were to become, and so had made a choice to go to school for many years: college, medical school, internship, residency, fellowship. The years add up: four plus four plus one plus two plus up to five. This is longer than it took the genie hotel to develop its business plan, longer than it took Aladdin to find his lamp.

My assignment at the conference was to work behind the scenes on a program that would report the current state-of-the-science about the hepatitis C virus and its treatment. Hepatitis C is a relatively recent discovery. When a surprise virus that attacked the liver made itself known in the mid-1970s, doctors asked, "What is this?" It wasn't hepatitis A, and it wasn't hepatitis B, names that doctors and even the public knew. It wasn't until 1989, after years of others trying and failing, that a group of researchers in California discovered the virus's true identity and gave it a name.

The men wore dark suits and ties. Their shirts were mostly white. The women wore dark jackets and skirts or slacks. A few bold women swirled a red or orange scarf across their shoulders. Like members of a club, they carried the same tote bag: navy canvas with black straps and an emblazoned logo.

The conference planners made the most of time. Inside each tote bag was a complimentary schedule showing a daily start time of 6:30 AM and end time of 8:30 PM.

During many of these hours, data from clinical trials were presented to audiences in 15-minute time slots, one after the other, or printed on posters and hung in an exhibit hall.

Hepatitis C keeps its own time. It gains quick access, blood to blood. A good number of people fight the virus with success, driving it out before it does damage, but for others the virus hides away in the liver. Viral particles, called virions, duplicate themselves at a rate of one trillion times per day for years and years. Liver damage accrues. Finally someone notices; the whites of the eyes yellow or a lab test comes back flagged.

Aladdin was the poor son of a poor tailor who had died when Aladdin was still a boy. One day, his fate changed when he found a magical lamp. He rubbed it and a genie appeared.

"Your wish is my command," the genie said to Aladdin.

As the bigger story goes, Scheherazade created the fairy tale of Aladdin and first told it to the Persian King Shahryar. It was one of many fairy tales that kept her alive. King Shahryar had the bad habit of marrying a woman and then killing her on their first matrimonial dawn, only to repeat the horror with his next betrothed. Along came Scheherazade, the newest fiancé, who knew she could outsmart the king. Her plan was this: tell the king a long story during the night but stop at the story's moment of climax, just before dawn.

Her plan worked! "Yes," said the king. "I want to hear how the story ends." He granted Scheherazade another day of life.

Scheherazade's cleverness continued. The next night she began another story immediately after finishing the first, adding an unexpected twist to coincide with the sun's rise. Again, the king was tricked. Again, he spared her life in exchange for the promise of the finished story. And so it went for many years until Scheherazade had told so many stories that she lived a long life and bore the king three sons.

Inside my hotel room, what a relief it had been to see a window. The hotel's elevator bay, lit with small silver neon lights, had been even darker than the lobby. In the hallway leading from the elevator to the room, only dim blue and green lights glowed. The room had white walls, two beds with mocha brown comforters, and an upholstered window seat with a folded navy blue blanket.

On the desk, adjacent to the window, a tray about one foot wide by two feet long held treats and sundry items, including a candy bar, a protein bar, a bag of chocolate peanut candies, a canister of potato chips, a mini-makeup kit, a music CD, and an "intimacy kit." The price list was buried, ensuring that wishes could be immediately granted without concern for cost. No need to call the front desk or scoot to the corner drug store. No need to pause to open a locked mini-bar. Take now.

On my first morning, I ordered room-service breakfast: granola, yogurt, and orange juice. The room steward delivered my tray.

"How do I get to the nearest pier on the bay?" I asked him as he turned to leave. Holding to the highest standards of customer service, he described the route, adding that the front desk offered guests a handy foldable map. "Just ask," he said with a smile that was used to granting wishes. Minutes later, I heard a knock on the door. There he stood, holding a map.

After an uneventful second morning, the third morning had me running late. Perhaps the hot water hadn't risen instantly into the shower head despite my wish that it would. Perhaps I had been daydreaming while washing and drying my hair.

"How long will granola and yogurt take?" I asked room service over the phone.

"Thirty minutes," said the woman, "but since you asked, I'll try for 20."

Wishes really could be commands in a place like this.

When I was a child, I had a book of stories that told its most intriguing story on the cover. It told a story about time. The glossy book board showed a picture of a little girl reading that very book of stories, with a picture of the same little girl on the cover reading that very book of stories, with a picture of that same little girl on the cover reading that very book of stories. How far out did this story go? Despite this hint of world without end, it seemed to take forever to eat an apple. I used to wonder, *is it worth the time from the moment of the first bite until the last?*

Lucky for me, I had been born to parents who were willing to invest in time along a broader dimension. They bought a library of reference books long before my sister or brother or I could even read, much less need them for reports on mountains and presidents, states and countries.

One after another, my father had pulled from boxes the new volumes of *The Encyclopedia Americana, The Book of Knowledge,* and *The Children's Classics,* which included Scheherazade's *Arabian Nights,* a volume with Aladdin's story. The once-upon-a-time's of *The Snow Queen, Robinson Crusoe,* and Persian fairy tales merged together with the population of Indiana, the history of ballet, and the discovery of penicillin as he placed the volumes side by side on the brick-and-board bookshelves he had built for our new brown suburban rambler with the big back yard and woods across the street.

Deep inside the world of test tubes, Petri dishes, incubators, and microscopes and long before non-A, non-B hepatitis was discovered to be hepatitis C, scientists learned how to slice, dice, and recombine deoxyribose nucleic acid, or DNA. They learned to inject this recombinant DNA into bacteria and make large amounts of various proteins, including interferon alfa.

Scientists tested interferon alfa in cultured cells, as well as in monkeys, mice, rats, and guinea pigs. They studied data from these tests to predict whether this protein could help people fight certain kinds of disease. The signs pointed to yes, and so interferon alfa began the multi-year drug development and clinical trial process for approval by the United States Food and Drug Administration, or FDA. Doctors began testing interferon alfa in small groups of people with hepatitis C. Next, it was tested on larger groups of people and for longer periods of time. After years of testing, the FDA approved interferon alfa for the treatment of hepatitis C.

Drug development and testing continued. In between milestones, smaller pieces of research fall into place: safety data here, subgroup efficacy analyses there. The body of knowledge moves forward by slow steps, with each step eagerly reported in 15-minute time slots by doctors and researchers at meetings all over the world. When completed steps reach a certain level of fullness, the data are gathered into a paper and submitted for publication. Over many years, more discoveries, including identification of the virus's genome and life cycle, and more trials with new anti-viral drugs, lead to even more effective approved therapies. The breakthrough that was interferon has now been nearly replaced. Drug development and testing continue even now.

The story of interferon, like so many advances in medicine, can be told thanks to a paper published in the April 25, 1953 issue of the journal *Nature*, "Molecular Structure of Nucleic Acids; a Structure for Deoxyribose Nucleic Acid." Its authors, James Watson and Francis Crick, won a firm place in history by their seminal discovery of the double-helix structure of DNA. People seem to forget, though, that the work of other scientists—Rosalind Franklin, Linus Pauling and Maurice Wilkins—was absorbed into this credit. The discovery won Watson, Crick, and Wilkins the 1962 Nobel Prize in Physiology or Medicine. In 1953 and 1962, neither Watson, Crick, Wilkins, Pauling, nor Franklin, nor the editors at *Nature*, nor the Nobel Prize committee members were concerned with or even knew about hepatitis C, yet the discovery of the structure of DNA nests inside the technology that allowed interferon alfa, its first approved treatment, to be made.

Most of the doctors and researchers involved in a poster or 15-minute study report wish to be in the place of Watson and Crick. They wish for their daily work to command a place in history.

Over time, Scheherazade's stories became so famous that they were gathered into a huge book named for the seemingly infinite number of stories she told, *The Book of One Thousand and One Nights.*

How easy it is to cheer for Aladdin, to long for the simple and immediate cause and effect. The control! How easy it is to overlook the real story: Scheherazade's slow and steady obedience to the strategy by which she daily purchased her life. A personal genie is so much more appealing than perpetual resourcefulness and courage, than imagination and patience, than active vulnerability to the nod of some other.

I think of a prayer written in my journal, repeated over pages and volumes. The dates change, racing forward. Oh, the longing for that wish to be granted. I have imagined a hand descending from the heavens, folding itself around my hand, and lifting the pen from its page. I imagine a voice whispering, *You can stop; it is time.*

The medical schools and accrediting bodies say "now" to the training doctors. The FDA says "now" to the drug researchers. Editors and historians say "now" to the authors of seminal papers. The calendar offers up the present moment to workers at their posts. The Maker of Time, in the fullness of time, says "now" to prayers for life and livelihood.

The story moves forward, and at the time when something must happen, the plot's accruing suspense does not disappoint. Continue, says Shahryar, and Scheherazade begins another of one thousand and one days. Is it the longer view or the present moment that she is attending?

The fourth morning at the genie hotel had been my last, and despite my wishes, there was no time for the usual granola and yogurt. Packing before the meeting's first session proved more difficult than expected. The volume of papers I had gathered during the meetings expanded beyond the space my luggage offered. I carried a stack of papers to the hotel's business office to be mailed home.

"Overnight, two-day, or standard?" asked the woman across the desk.

"Two-day is fine," I responded, not wanting to be too commanding.

Later that day, I flew back across two time zones to my Midwestern city, far from bays and piers. I unpacked. Out of my briefcase came papers, pens, the conference book of abstracts, and my schedule. Out of my suitcase came my black skirt and black tights, brown pants and brown shoes, hair dryer and brush. Out of my handbag came my book, *Confessions* by St. Augustine, a book written in the fourth century by a man whose life changed on a dime that had been spinning for years, a book that I had read in snatched moments in my hotel room on the window seat flooded with light. About the Maker of Time, Augustine wrote, "Your years are as a single day; and Your day comes not daily but is today, a today which does not yield place to any tomorrow or follow upon any yesterday. In you today is eternity...." Ancient words travel time and hit their mark.

Prompted by my stay at the genie hotel, I went to my bookshelf to look for and read that inherited *Arabian Nights*. At the time of the book's purchase, more than five decades ago, what would my parents, then a young couple, have thought if they had realized they were investing in stories that would be opened again after lying latent for so long? Could they have known that their planning and action would have a yield so far into the future? They must have had some hint—or was it a wish?—that time would yet require something of their investment, because as this volume sits on my shelf its broken binding is held together with transparent tape carefully placed years ago by hands other than my own.

Kairos pierces chronos.

SEVENTEEN
Centripetal Centrifugal Counterpoise

ON REIMAGINING WORK

T ry doodling a labyrinth in a memo's margin or over a filled calendar square. Start at the center with a symmetrical Greek cross, two lines of equivalent length intersecting at their midpoints. Now widen your view and place this cross inside an imaginary square. Draw four inverted corners where the corners of that square would be, pointing each toward the center. Widen your view a bit more and draw four dots at the corners of a still larger imaginary square. Working from left to right, draw arcs connecting line to line, line to dot, dot to line, line to line, line to line, line to dot, dot to line, line to line until it looks like a mushroom and then a brain, and the circuitous path of ancient pilgrims opens to your visit.

Once, I came across a labyrinth on a hill far from home. It was my first. A couple years earlier, I had tried dragging my finger along the arcs of a finger labyrinth I found in a basket next to me as I sat alone in a chapel trying to pray, but the finger dragging produced no great spiritual effect. I suspect I did it wrong, looking for that final cause end result that would qualify the preceding experience as worthwhile. The receptive meditative state I failed to achieve and the dashed hope that my fingers would channel some sort of message reminded me of when I was one of several sixth-grade girls at a slumber party playing with a disallowed Ouija board— disallowed then by my mother's rule and disallowed now by my own understanding of the basis of that rule. "What's the name of the boy I'm going to marry?" we took turns asking with nervous giggles. Nonsense responses of jumbled letters emerged for each of us in turn as our fingers nervously rode the planchette around the board. We knew even then that futures were hidden.

Inward, toward the labyrinth's center, I placed each foot in turn—right, left, right—on the red paver stones that formed its path. No expectations: I'd walk it, that's all. Hurry through. An afternoon rain was stepping over the horizon, and in my back-pack a Snickers bar with almonds softened in the high heat. Green pavers traced the perimeter of the circular whole and filled the interstices between the path's switchback turns.

I tried not to look ahead or anticipate the directional flips, back and forth, around and around, that prevented you from ever being able to predict with certainty where you were headed and when you would arrive. I looked only where my foot was about to land. It seemed a necessary discipline. A few months earlier, I'd read Jean-Pierre de Caussade's *The Sacrament of the Present Moment*. Its call to attend to the here and now still pressed upon me for under-standing, "Our souls can only be truly nourished, strengthened, enriched, and sanctified by the bounty of the present moment. What more can we ask?"

North, then south; west, then east; then north again. No star-tling insights bubbled up as I walked. Shall I blame the loud wom-en and children talking and playing at the labyrinth's entrance? Was it me, hurrying to avoid the rain, hungry for the chocolate I car-ried? Or was it just the way it is? Long paths and turn, turn, turn, and still no clue, no why as to the direction change, no seeming progress toward a hidden destination, but still you keep walking because a place is provided on which to step next, and so you go.

The day ahead often reads like an unopened book. Its outline is apparent, but you can't know its twists and turns. Sometimes I'm afraid of it. On my wedding day, my grandfather—he in his dark suit, I in my long white dress—recited words from an old poem to me, ever so quietly and gently, "Go out into the darkness and put your hand into the hand of God. That shall be to you better than light and safer than a known way."

You can walk this path forever—inward and outward and in-ward again—rather than stepping away, through and beyond the exit, and always keep hoping for how the story will end because it never ends until it's over. Often I think I've figured out a story's conclusion in advance but then find that I've been wrong, as if by grabbing hold of one end of the narrative thread I could see where the other end finally anchors and trace the in between.

When you get to the center of a labyrinth, you can't see the cross that was drawn to seed the structure. There is only a space. The center may be no bigger than the circumference of an average adult, but it is a place of hospitality. You can stay as long as you want.

Some time after the labyrinth on the hill, I came upon one mowed into a small field. At the intersection of the arms of the Greek cross was a hard desk chair. I sat in it and thought awhile. The path had led to a spacious place. I closed my eyes and turned my face to the afternoon sun.

It's easy to confuse the center of a labyrinth for a dead-end if you don't see that the way out is to just get back on the path.

I have told this story before in other renditions, but I keep going over and over the plot line in words, writing back and forth toward a destination, trying to connect the dots. Story meets reverie, and we make sense of our way. Dreams of freedom had been filling my head. That's the effect scribbling notes in the margins has on me. I don't want the margins to stop. Get on any highway; stay on it long enough and it will take you out of town, beyond city limits, over the horizon.

Here was the plan: cut back on paid client work and let my husband's earnings cover most of the bills while I write my own words, at least for awhile. There were all kinds of good reasons for this plan, not the least of which was a mysterious conflation of events and inner sensation that bore the voiceprint of call issued from a realm beyond. I wanted to respond, to answer. I wanted to call back.

About this plan, my husband agreed with smiles and cheers. Someday it would happen. We waited.

Then, after turbulent years of my husband's un- and underemployment and job searching, that "someday" appeared to arrive. Secure in a new job and with more than a year under his belt plus an early promotion, he was earning enough for me to let go of the majority household income demands. "Start turning down some work projects," he said.

We were still flush with peace over the start of this new phase in life, only days into it, when he came home late with the news delivered in the dark kitchen, the hushed choked news of job loss. The wrong card drawn yet again.

Within a week, I said "yes" to three new paying projects. *Responsibility*, Bonhoeffer reminds. My husband—devastated, devastated—typed up a new resume and began again the search for a job. The years drag on.

The road forward turns back on itself with no apparent progress made, and here we are again where we started, looping back in time like an airplane loops back in space spirally along a Rhumb line track between departure and arrival. If de Caussade had been in that kitchen when the job news was delivered, he would likely have put his arm around our shoulders in camaraderie with that moment's sacrament—and surrender.

A labyrinth's exit and entrance are one and the same, depending on what you do with it. You can call it quits or pivot and start again inward toward the center.

Far from the labyrinth on the hill, I'm walking today with my sunglasses on, though the day is cloudy. Compounding work crises carry the weight of the proverbial last straw that, if not actually breaking the camel's back, forces compression cracks and pain.

Don't cry at work, the experts tell you; I work at home yet heed the advice. I once worked for a hard boss who kept a box of tissues in a drawer by the guest chair in her office. She could open that drawer in one fluid and cruel motion that told me many had sat in her office and succumbed to tears. I'm walking it off, blinking it back, letting things settle and pack down so there is room inside for more.

I've wanted to quit the work for hire in response to a perceived call, but the path under my feet hasn't allowed it. How can peace be made?

Two morning devotional readings compete for my attention. From Ecclesiastes, a question and a complaint, "What do people get from all the toil and anxious striving with which they labor under the sun? All their days their work is grief and pain; even at night their minds do not rest." And from a pilgrimage Psalm, a blessing, "Blessed are those whose strength is in you, whose hearts are set on pilgrimage." Walking, I bounce from one reading to the other, murmuring grievances with the commiseration of the first reading, quieting myself with the hope in the second.

How can peace be made? The only way that comes to me now is to expand the perceived call's range, to imagine anew how it can play out.

Take off the sunglasses, dry both eyes, and sit down again at the desk. Hold the reading of complaint in the left hand and the reading of hope in the right. In this desk chair is the place where I live. In this office is the field where I attend to Life. In this field, whether chosen or given, a treasure has been hidden and the game to find it is on.

If the world can be seen in a hazelnut, then who I am and what I am to be about can be seen in any and every moment. Here is my sense of mercy, love, and justice; here is how I treat another; here is where I am healed, and in turn, offer healing; here is everything

I ever learned; here is everything laid bare; here is where I walk humbly with my God.

Blur the distinction between life and work. It's all of one piece unless you don't allow it to be. Cast your gaze over anything—let your view widen—over even this field of work, and what you see growing is Life, with meaning everywhere to be cultivated. Hope, wrote Peter Berger, signals a reality beyond reality.

Carry the chair in the sun, the still point, inside, I tell myself. Simone Weil wrote of a center outside of time and space, a center that is the intersection of created and Creator, the point of intersection of the arms of the cross. Our Father, thy kingdom come; thy will be done on earth as it is in heaven. Writing about work, I'm in perpetual Lent. Something is always being given up with the expectation of something more to come. Here now at work, to the cross and back: obedience and surrender. Weil and de Caussade and Bonhoeffer trump the motivational speakers reveling in bliss. In the tension between chosen and given, wisdom on the flip side of career savvy comes calling.

Uphold me; sustain me; guard me; teach me; Lord have mercy. The center will hold no other way. This moment of prayer informs all others, bridging as it does one reality with another: the reality of the press of the foot on pavement with the reality of the Spirit who leads and beckons and breathes in life. Its force pulls me in, then spins me back out.

≈

Outside the perimeter of the labyrinth on the hill, two men wearing suits stood talking. I heard them as I took a turn.

"Because there's no hedge you don't even have to walk it," said one man to the other. "You can just follow it through with your eyes and see where it goes."

Neither the Camino de Santiago nor the Appalachian Trail, this pilgrimage is mine. It began with my last failed plan yet dates back to my first passage through the door of a job. It takes me from project to project—not from relic to relic, or season to season, or outpost to outpost. If I don't step away, I just might figure out ways to understand Life through the labor. There may be more of us that need to make peace with staying on a path than there are those who should step away to something new. Even Thoreau had to leave Walden and return to selling pencils. Staying in place is a pilgrimage too.

This walking and turning and walking again takes time. It's tempting to jump ahead with a glance—or a wish—and skip the here and now steps along the physical stone path. It's tempting to step away, to step to the perimeter and join the suited men who hold back their bodies from the next step and the next, substituting instead a quick assessment from a safe distance. It's tempting to ride our mental planchettes around the various possibilities of how things will play themselves out. In reality, though, only two options exist: walk through or step away.

I recently read that you first must find out who you are in order to find work you love. That notion, ideal and lovely when talking to a college senior in a career counseling office, too easily glosses over another reality: wrestling with work, love it or not; rising back up after the match but, like Jacob, walking away with a limp; discovering only then an identity for yourself you never knew and the identity of the actual partner against whom you wrestled.

My husband has found a job at the small gym down our street. Far from who he thought he was, he now manages machines that can make you strong and the gym's members who use them. It's not quite full time, and there is no health insurance or 401K, but it is something. More than something. It seems we can't go anywhere without running into someone who knows him from the gym and gives him a wave or stops to talk. We smile at his popularity. Behind the smile is the ongoing job search for the work he'd rather be doing that's still beyond his reach.

I may not have ever walked a labyrinth before, but I knew this much: your feet must touch the path laid before them, your fingers slicing the air as they move, your body one step further and another. Your eyes may not be able to see beyond where you are now, and that must sometimes be enough. I'm practicing not glossing over the little words that pop up in the Psalms now and again in the Orthodox version I sometimes read, "So be it."

EIGHTEEN
Body of Work

ON THE HOPE OF BROKENNESS

What is this body that walks into the office and sits down at the desk, this body that shows up for another day of work, another round of Life? Breath and blood, flesh and brain, heart and bones. The two-dimensional resume fails this asset.

Lately I have been palpating flesh to feel bone's density and outline, trying to picture its marrow, the caverns, and the channels deep inside, hidden beneath the external hardness. I have been thinking about bone, writing about bone. Worrying about bone.

On my work desk is a project about bone health in the setting of cancer. As if people with cancer don't have enough to worry about with cellular division gone awry, they also must worry about the deep aching pain, fractures, and nerve compression that comes when malignant cells spread to bone. Like a piece of dead coral you can find on a beach, bone becomes porous and weak. Put some pressure on it and listen for the crack; feel the break. For these patients—"patient" from the Latin *patiens,* meaning to suffer—the goals are to control the pain and strengthen the bone. As God challenged Ezekiel in the valley of dry bones, *Can these bones live?* Sometimes this writing is like watching the thousandth news segment about a war or natural disaster, and you have to shake yourself or splash cold water on your face to see it as about something real.

What is real is that my teenage son has fallen while working, and he has broken some bones. Amid the papers on my desk about bone health in cancer are workman's compensation forms, notes from doctor's appointments and calls. A compact disc contains black and white radiographic images of the ulna and radius, the wrist's scaphoid, lunate, triquetrum, trapezium, trapezoid, capitate, and hamate bones. He braced a long fall with his right hand, the hand with which he signs his name. It was his second day at a summer construction job. How lucky, he thought, to have this chance to make good money.

The construction site was a house with a high cathedral ceiling. My son stood on a scaffold within the ceiling's cavity, hammering framework in place. I picture him—suntanned in T-shirt and paint-splotched jeans, blond buzzed hair—with hammer in hand, shoulder drawing back then forearm swinging forward as wrist pivots to knock hammer against wood. Over and over, his muscles sustain the rhythm. Summer sweat drips down his forehead, but he doesn't take his eyes off the wood.

I see what he doesn't. The scaffold separates from the wall more and more with each swing before it finally breaks away, dropping him nine feet onto a cement floor. I try not to picture him falling.

∼

Nearly 10 hours of surgery marked my son with a four-inch vertical scar down the side of his hand starting at the base of the thumb; a two-inch horizontal scar on the topside of his wrist; a six-inch vertical scar starting at the underside of his wrist and down his forearm. Higher up on his forearm is an older scar from his previous summer's work as a painter. An electric sander caught his glove and worked its way through to his skin before he could free himself.

I have two scars, fewer and smaller, but in similar places. A half-inch horizontal scar that shimmers when it catches the light lies rooted at the base of my right thumb. I don't remember the cause, only that it hurt while as a child I watched it bleed. The second scar is from a surgery that placed two screws at the base of a broken thumb, leaving a two-inch vertical scar along the inside of that thumb as if the flesh had been embroidered with a thread of pale pink silk.

One surgery fixed my hand. My son's hand required three, and "fixed" would be a less than accurate verb.

"I think we have a problem," said the surgeon after looking at the first set of X-rays one week after the first surgery. A bone had rotated out of position.

"I think we have a problem," said the surgeon after looking at the next set of X-rays four weeks after the second surgery. The same bone had again rotated.

The damage from the fall was deeper than we had known. A 5,000 dollar set of CAT and MRI scans revealed two more breaks and one piece of bone wedged far from its rightful place.

The third surgery lasted more than four hours. My husband and I were the only ones left in the waiting room by the time it was over. The receptionist had said good-bye, turned off the coffee maker, and walked out the door, leaving us to watch *Frasier* reruns on the television hanging from the wall.

The surgeon strode into the room wearing his blue surgical scrubs, bonnet, and booties. Tucked under his arm was an unvarnished wooden box. He sat down next to me and placed the box on the table between us, dropping his Lexus car keys on top. He drew three pictures showing the incisions he made, the bones and ligaments he joined, and the places where pins holding bones together were now temporarily sticking out of my son's wrist.

My eyes followed his drawing but skipped over to the box. Six faded and partially abraded stickers of pink girlish cartoon characters decorated its top. Out from under some memory rock came another box from my surgery. In the recovery room, the surgeon had stood by my bed holding a wooden box, and from my post-anesthesia haze I had asked him about it. A gift from his father, he said. What the box held, I couldn't remember.

The X-ray images, taken three days after my son's third surgery, were suitable for framing. The surgeon beamed. A matrix of bones, rows and columns, like a double-rowed pearl bracelet, one articular surface meeting another, is a beautiful sight, and no less beautiful when aided by screws and pins and sutures. Now we would wait.

In an act of paradox as contrary as any, bone breaks itself down to build itself up. Sensors deep in the bone detect fractures, even the quotidian fatigue crack you might not notice. A chemical signal triggers one type of cell to burrow out weakened bone and another type of cell to fill it back in with stronger bone. Hidden deep below my son's scar, a flurry of growth swirled.

Even in the absence of a fracture, this process of breaking down and building up goes on. Like a bank, bone is in the business of molecular deposits and withdrawals with calcium as the currency. Calcium from the stars, calcium from milk and green leafy vegetables and chalky white pills yields more than strong bones. The heart stops beating, nerves stop transmitting, and muscles stop contracting without it. To provide the needed calcium, bone issues a withdrawal through a complex cycle of chemical reactions, breaking itself down in the process. When the body's calcium supply is sufficient, bone accepts a deposit, building itself back up. Without this continuous intrinsic remodeling, there is no vitality in the body, no strength of inner being.

Days later, the surgeon removed the surgical dressing. He began snipping stitches, then stopped and left the room.

He returned with the wooden box, still gilded with the cartoon stickers. From it he lifted surgical glasses, thick black frames with a magnifier appendage projecting from each lens. I remembered then that my surgeon's box had also held glasses. He seated them across his nose and over his ears and proceeded to finish his work.

Our task now was to be patient as the stabilized bone worked to heal and strengthen itself with its invisible exchanges. Once, years ago and at the close of one work project, which had not been easy, and at the start of another, the ease of which we did not yet know, the project director borrowed words of the psalmist, "We go from strength to strength."

The structural soundness of my son's hand didn't last. Two months after the third surgery and back at college, he called from across the country. Another X-ray had been taken. "The bone rotated again," he said. A new orthopedic specialist is on the case. He's not quite sure what is next. "Get the wrist moving, get another CAT scan; then we can see where we are," he said.

The injury will stay with my son in ways that we can't yet know. I can type without reminder of the injury underneath my second scar. When I write longhand, however, with my scarred thumb anchoring the proximal side of a pen, the tension of the grip and the bend of the joints often strains this not-quite-whole thumb more than it can bear. A few lines and the ache simmers, the cramp bubbles up and must be stirred down with a drop of the pen and a shake of the hand.

What is this body that shows up for another day of work, another round of Life, this bundle of complexity marked by the tattooing of experience, by remodeling and emergency fixes, by aches that lie bound to natural healing or man-made screws?

Don the spectacles and look down deep. Blood pulses; nerves fire. Travel the inner topography of scar, over and around which the mind roves; our inner contours remodeled time and time again on the way to strength. Briefcases and messenger bags can't possibly zip themselves around what we bring to the table.

For the rest of his life, my son will look at his right hand and see the evidence of break and incision and stitching. His hand emerges like a flower from this calyx of sepal scars. The work of his hand will be anchored by this whorl.

We are writing our bodies of work.

What beauty will arise?

NINETEEN
Physiology Lessons

ON HOW THINGS WORK TOGETHER

I have been collecting images, lifting layers, switching between depths of field to catch glimpses of what's really going on here. How does work become more than what it is, and how do we become ourselves in the process? How do we find livelihood even as we are making it? How can an individual body of work contribute to a corporate body of work to participate in a universal, eternal, world-without-end body of work?

On my bookshelf sits a slim volume with a hard cover the color of blood. This anatomy book belonged to my mother in her nursing school days. Tucked into the book's middle and flanked by pages heavy with text are pages of drawings created by a master medical illustrator using colored pencils or paints. As a child, I made a beeline for these pages. Here, I could look at a heart with its valves and chambers or run my finger over the brain with its lobes. I could see how a baby curled up tight inside a woman's belly.

My favorite drawings were those of the head-to-toe human body, one Mylar overlay on top of another and another so that by lifting one layer at a time you could go deeper and deeper inside and see what this body was made of. Lift the first layer, and you strip off the skin, revealing the pink criss-crossing striations of muscle wrapped over shoulders and around wrists alike. Lift another layer, and trace blood vessels, colored red and blue, thin as string, that bleed in real life when cut. Lift another, and see the shiny liver and labyrinthine intestines. Lift one more, and uncover the bones, white and chalky.

I sometimes sat with my mother on her bed and asked her how it all worked, these parts of a whole and the whole together with its parts.

Sacrament comes from the Latin, *sacramentum*, a translation of the Greek word for mystery. Augustine famously defined sacrament as a visible sign of an invisible grace. Years ago I copied out words from a Lenten book into my journal, "Pray to remember that upon you rest both the favor of God and the power of the Spirit." This is how I think of God's grace coming to us. And these words, "dedicate with faith your personal lifelong pilgrimage—regardless of how insignificant it may seem to you—as an important part of God's liberation of the world." This is how I think of God's grace flowing through us. Even so, I easily forget about grace—coming to, flowing through—because it is invisible and even imagining it is hard work sometimes.

Please, Augustine, show me the signs.

I have felt bread on the tongue and water on flesh, but I crave signs of grace outside the cloister of the sanctuary and so am drawn to a teacher's recent suggestion to try living all of life as a sacrament, as a physical participation in the flow of grace from God to people and among people and back again. This suggestion is virtually the same as that made by de Caussade back in 1751 in *The Sacrament of the Present Moment,* but explained this way, without the minute-by-minute reminder of duty, is easier to smile along to. Who wouldn't sign up to live like that, in the flow of grace coming and going?

My life, your life, as visible signs of invisible grace.

Then I remember Christ's life and how it wasn't always something to smile along to, and I sober up. The surface view of grace isn't synonymous with the good life; history bears that out. Sometimes the favor and power of God, the share in God's liberation of the world looks like sweaty hard work, failed work even. I have to wonder about my willingness to live sacramentally, my willingness to have headaches and high blood pressure, frustration and exhaustion be visible signs of invisible grace as God works in me and through me.

My eye of understanding needs a face, and I think often of my friend Colette. She had wanted the labor that would birth her seventh child to be easy. If you asked anyone who knew her, they would have agreed that she deserved an easy labor. She planned to have an epidural to numb the nerves waist down to spare herself the pain, to free herself to enjoy the experience in a way that she had not in her previous five labors. When the time came, however, the midwife said no to the epidural. The baby was breech and up too far.

I asked her about the labor when I visited her afterward and got to hold Veronica, three weeks old and wrapped in a powder-pink blanket. Colette sat next to me on the couch holding the family dog, her brown hair pulled back in a ponytail, her brown eyes serene and joyful. She wore an orange short-sleeved knit shirt and khaki pants with a set-in zipper, impressive so soon after delivery.

"So how was it?"

"Painful and hard," she said then paused. "But sweet and peaceful."

Cradled in my arms, Veronica wore a long-sleeved bodysuit of robins-egg blue knit adorned with lavender flowers that snapped along the front and down her legs. Her peachy complexion sparkled against the wardrobe pastels, like a gold coin in the sand glittering back to the sun.

The day of delivery had been a Thursday in Lent, three weeks before Holy Thursday, three weeks and one day before Good Friday. With each contraction, Colette recited part of a prayer said in her church starting at 3 PM on Good Friday, the hour associated with Jesus's death, "For the sake of His sorrowful Passion, have mercy on us and on the whole world."

Thinking about it now, Colette's prayer and intention to journey beside Jesus, linking her contractions to his suffering, reminds me of a scene in Georges Bernanos's *The Diary of a Country Priest*. The Curé of Torcy, an elder, a mentor, is sharing a notion of his with the young priest, who has long been discouraged and sick. He imagines that in some sort of time warp that presents no problem to time's maker, each of us meets Jesus long before we are born somewhere on his road from Bethlehem to Golgotha. Our eyes and his lock, and that is the place of calling. *There are words for you alone.* For the elder priest, the place was Mount Olivet where Jesus asked Peter and the rest of the disciples, *Why sleep ye?*

Colette furrowed her brow for me as she finished saying the prayer. The space above her nose and between her eyes came together in small tight folds. "Whenever my forehead tightened like this my labor coach would rub it with her thumb to remind me to relax and pray," she said, demonstrating the rubbing and relaxing.

At the Sixth Station of the Cross, tradition has it that as Jesus carried his cross to Golgotha, it was Veronica who broke through the crowd and wiped his face after he fell, before he fell again. Veronica, risking physical censure by the Roman guards, lifted her hands to his tightened furrowed brow and brought her veil down upon his skin, absorbing the tears, blood, sweat, and spit.

Bernanos's troubled young priest dared not admit he was forever linked to the agony of Gethsemane. Others might conclude Jesus rested his eyes on them when he calmed the sea, or rubbed his spit in dirt to bring sight to a man's eyes, or gathered up the children, or taught on a mountaintop, or worked in his father's carpentry shop, or turned water into wine at a party.

"Lord have mercy" prayers have been streaming in my head like a subliminal tape, and I am being remodeled in the process. Lord have mercy: on the sender of that email, that work client, that colleague, or more times than I care to admit, on me.

My imagination often starves for the signs of grace to be unveiled in the realm of my work. I understand that by writing documents about treatment strategies and disease management, my place is on the healing team, but who are my patients and where exactly is healing transacted? From my desk, I never see the face of a person who is diagnosed, treated, or cured. I write the same disease statistics over and over again, but figures in the range of seven to nine digits don't quickly budge. I forget what is possible.

Massimo Camisasca wrote, "Every action, seen through God's eyes, has an infinite echo, it unleashes an atomic reaction that will never end, that brings the moment to eternity, to the infinite." Pick a letter, any letter, from this computer's keyboard. The path arcs upward with each tap. The world in a hazelnut; Christ in a key; love in a word. An eternal echo in a PowerPoint slide? Given that vision, how dare I not dip my fingers in holy water before doing the work for which I'll later pass my hat for my pay? Who knows what can happen.

There's an ancient story about Gideon that I like. Gideon found himself talking to an angel of the Lord. The angel sat with him and sent him to be a warrior. "Go in the strength you have," he told Gideon, the weakest family member in the weakest clan. Gideon asked the angel to wait while he went to get an offering, and he returned with unleavened bread, a pot of broth, and a basket of meat. The tip of the angel's staff touched the bread and meat laid out on a rock. From the rock, fire flashed to set the offering ablaze.

Lord have mercy: on this project, the clinicians who will read it, the sick they will treat, the pharmacists who will dispense, the employers who will insure, the families who will support, the researchers, laboratory technologists, statisticians, trial nurses, phlebotomists. The have-mercies could go on forever once the path starts and the circle and webs and intersections present themselves. T. S. Eliot wrote,

> And what you thought you came for
> Is only a shell, a husk of meaning
> From which the purpose breaks only when it is fulfilled
> If at all.

After 40 days of Lent, the moment arrives on Easter Sunday when "Hallelujah" is spoken again for the first time:

The Lord is risen.

The Lord is risen indeed, Hallelujah.

"As loudly as you can," the minister encourages, and the congregation to which I belong responds as loudly as our Minnesota sensibility allows.

This church doesn't have an organ, but in other churches of which I've been a part, Easter Sunday closes with a pipe organ driving forward the "Hallelujah" chorus. The organist seals the service of resurrection with 12 pages of chords, each made up of nearly as many notes as fingers, played to a metronome pace of *allegro*: fast, lively. The neurobiology of music has theories to explain the tingle, the shiver, I feel whenever I hear this chorus, theories that involve nerve stimulation, changes in heart rate and blood flow, inhibition of some parts of the brain and activation of others. Frisson evoked by music has everything to do with expectation, says musicologist David Huron, and is not so different from that evoked by fear.

My mother had a tattered musical score of Handel's *Messiah* left over from years of singing in church choirs. I've practiced its music on the piano, first on the maple spinet in my parents' living room while I was in high school and still taking piano lessons, and later in my own house on an inherited upright. But Handel's music exceeds my reach. My fingers stumble across the keys. The first movement, "Overture," with its single F-sharp offers the most success. Here is where I start each time I try again. With fingers warm and confidence boosted, I progress to the air for alto, "He Shall Feed His Flock Like A Shepherd," and then back to the chorus, "And The Glory of The Lord." The chords corresponding to that chorus' final drawn out words—"hath spoookeen iit"—jettison me toward the oratorio's climax: the "Hallelujah" chorus. On those pages, stumbling fingers meet frisson in a strange sensation of participating in something I know not what, in expectation of I know not what, but always with the hope that it would somehow include a miraculous transformation of my inadequate, but earnest, music making.

I am collecting images, lifting layers, switching between depths of field to catch glimpses of what's really going here, to understand how all things work together, and here is a show not to be missed. One December, I went to the Cathedral of St. Paul in St. Paul's Summit Hill neighborhood to hear the Minnesota Orchestra and Minnesota Chorale perform *Messiah*, conducted by Eiji Oue, the Orchestra's music director at the time. My memory of this evening from years ago is tinted golden, like the Cathedral's low lighting reflecting off its gold-leafed dome. Perfume of gilded women and cologne of suited men blended with the incense of Sundays past to compose an aromatic combination as heady as any a master perfumer could create. The tuning notes of the oboes and flutes, clarinets and trumpets, violins and cellos accompanied the clatter and shuffle of high heels and leather soles on marble flooring as people found their seats.

Across the risers behind the orchestra, the chorale members filed in and took their places. The orchestra members straightened their backs and placed their instruments across their laps. Oue entered.

Applause! Applause!

He turned to face his singers, then lifted his baton and held it still. Now the nave was silent, like a bedroom in the moment before its sleeper awakens. The baton bobbed and with that, the story set to music hit its first note. The joined groups began at the same place as any stumbling piano player or church choir, with the "Overture." Except for one intermission, they continued straight through the oratorio to the final adagio "Amen," performing not only the sections related to Advent, the arias and choruses of the prophets and angels, but also the sections related to Lent and Easter, the laments of crucifixion and the celebration of resurrection.

When the moment came for the shout withheld, not for 40 days but 43 sections, the audience stood in the tradition said to have begun with King George II. The musicians did not disappoint. Ten times in unison the chorale exploded the pent up, "Hallelujah." Forward they went, pushing the crescendo upward. Oue nearly danced, body swaying and arms swinging left, right, diagonally, up, down.

Then, he stopped.

My memory is that it happened just after the sopranos hit the high A in the round of echoes, "and He shall reign for ever and ever." Oue lowered his arms, clasped his hands together behind his back, and lifted his face toward the singers.

He stood still.

I couldn't take my eyes off of him. Wasn't this his moment of glory, carrying his sopranos and tenors, his violinists and cellists, and his audience to the height of sublimity?

The painted dove in flight saw it all from above on the dome's inner surface, ringed below with paintings and stained glass. I read later about the Cathedral, that the paintings are images of the gifts of the Spirit—knowledge, counsel, understanding, piety, fear of the Lord, fortitude, and wisdom—and that the windows depict the Sacraments of Baptism, Reconciliation, Eucharist, Confirmation, Matrimony, Holy Orders, and Anointing of the Sick.

The voices soared, propelled by the strings, horns, woodwinds, and percussion. Upward to the dome. Careening around the marble curves. Bursting the bronze. Oue, however, remained still, his arms and hands restrained, his baton at rest. No assuring gesticulations to his performers, no cues aiming for perfection, no rhythmic pounding out of time. The show went on without him. At this climax of the climax, he revealed what had been concealed, like the magician who dares to show the trick the eye had been too slow to see.

The visible evidence of the invisible grace that powered the show ricocheted off the painted dove and crashes years later into my starved imagination. With the baton drawn down, the surface layer of effort, sweat, and skill removed, you get the hint that anything can happen. With grace flowing—in and through—who knows how high the voices will finally rise, how far the sound will carry, what beauty will shine? In the spirit of Ecclesiastes, there is a time to work and a time to let it go. When we say the word we're meant to say or do the deed we're meant to do, pray to God that it moves beyond the cloister of the workspace. Release it; by grace may it rise and carry and shine. Hope that it catches a current and rides to places unknown. Hope that even a leaf might move from a sigh sighed in ordinary time. By grace may it heal.

In my memory, Oue waits out the extended nine-beat final "*Hallelujah,*" not bringing his work through to completion by his own sweat, not receiving the grateful and euphoric gaze of his singers and players in the flush of accomplishment. In my memory, his head, by then, is bowed; but in fact, it may be that the head bowed is my own.

∾

The weigela bushes are the latest object of my neighbor Bob's attention. Their fuchsia flowers are still weeks from bursting, the green buds new last week. He has fertilized them on schedule, and their springtime resurrection proceeds. With shovel in hand, he aims at the ground around each base, places a foot and steps down. The blade pierces the ground. He pushes on the shovel's handle, lifts the dirt, and turns it over. The roots need space and fresh air. He repeats down the row, topping with mulch.

The lawn is waking up, now twice as green as yesterday despite a heavy thatch of brown. Still, there is enough grass that two rabbits have been finding sufficient sustenance to warrant grazing the last few evenings. They are surprisingly plump after their long hibernation. Along the back of the fence, shrubs are stick bouquets awaiting buds and blossoms. Ferns lay furled underground. Lilac blooms are a month away. Two Adirondack chairs face southwest, the best position to catch the afternoon sun. All is empty now, but open. All is expectant. A yellow day-lily, underground, bides its time in this neutral moment before the concert begins.

TWENTY
Portrait Gallery

ON *IMAGO DEI* AND COUNTENANCE

Up one level from the museum's main floor, just beyond the darkness of the adjacent gallery, the light and beauty of this gift shop burst upon you like a paradise you never expected. I've brought guests and, stepping over the threshold, have heard their gasp. The shop is part of The Museum of Russian Art, which is in my neighborhood and housed in a Spanish Colonial Revival-style building that was at first a church and then a mortuary before an art collector with a vision, an architect, and a work crew redeemed it.

Taking a break from work, I walked the few blocks to buy a birthday gift there. Ironically named for a peasant's hut, *The Izba* has white walls, dark wood accents, Romanesque windows, and a high ceiling. Tables and shelves display textiles, cards and books, lacquer boxes, jewelry, textiles, pottery, and china. Paintings and icons hang on its walls.

The salesclerk, a middle-aged man with wire-frame glasses, thinning hair, an oval face, fair skin, and a gentle smile saw me wandering the aisles with a cup of complimentary hot blueberry tea in my hand. He caught my eye and invited me to watch him and his assistant unpack the new icons, merchandise to reflect their current exhibit, "Transcendent Art: Icons from Yaroslavl, Russia."

"Come and see," he said.

Past the rack of amber and silver earrings and around the locked case of gems and porcelain beyond my price range, one icon was already laid out on a glass counter. About the dimensions and heft of a large coffee table book, the icon was an image of Mary encased in a metal cover, an *oklad*, silver with brushstrokes of gold, its relief design one of chasing and repoussé. Through windows excised from the metal, I could see her face and hands. The Virgin held her baby, and her armor opened also for his face and his diminutive hands and feet. Another opening the size of a shelled pistachio nut laid bare his torso. Whether the opening intended to reveal his heart or to-be-pierced side, I couldn't be sure.

Two years earlier, this museum curated a smaller icon exhibit. Dr. Wendy Salmond, a scholar of Russian and early Soviet art, gave a lecture about icons to anyone who wanted knowledge about the form and practice beyond what the exhibit offered. I sat in the audience in the museum's basement lecture room. Salmond told the history of icon making: how it had been a sacred art practiced in near monastic fashion in specific villages in Russia but made illegal with the 1917 Bolshevik revolution. Bonfires fueled by confiscated wooden icons expunged the opiate of the masses. By decree, the new regime de-sacralized the work of the artists and offered lacquer boxes as the non-negotiable alternative, like a parent pulling messy paints away from a child and offering crayons instead.

Here is what made icons dangerous: they claimed to be a divine witness to human affairs. Call them a conduit. They hinted of more than meets the eye—metal cases that shield and adorn, painted eyes with flat facial expressions, distorted dimensions of setting. Pierce their veils, and meet God.

Icons reminded people, Salmond said, that we are always on the brink of a higher reality. I took the reminder seriously, hungrily even, and wrote the words in my notebook, setting them alongside all the other words I'd written therein and thereabouts as if in joint supplication. I write of things about which I do not know, at least not fully. I see through a glass darkly, the same as St. Paul, but oh how I try. Polish the glass and stare long and hard, hoping to catch movement on the other side, a reflection of this world against the next.

Salmond showed a slide of the 1881 painting by Vasilii Maksimov called "The Sick Husband." The scene is set in a Russian peasant's home; wood planks form the floor, walls, and ceiling; clothes hang from pegs. An old man lies wrapped in blankets on a straw mattress supported by a wood frame. Boots topple underneath. Next to him is a bench with bottles that I imagine are tinctures and remedies. Fabric covers the only window, yet light as from a spotlight enters from somewhere outside the picture's frame. Above the man and woman is a shelf of framed icons, their subjects each with eyes wide.

Face-to-face beholdings sneak up on you. At a restaurant a few blocks north of Chicago's Magnificent Mile and a few blocks east of Lake Michigan's West shore, we diners ate our soup, our chili, our chicken and salads surrounded by a cloud of witnesses, but we hardly noticed for our hunger and chatter. Music from the sixties and seventies—Doobie Brothers, The Beatles, Fleetwood Mac—blared; revolving glass doors spun men, women, and children in from the street and out; people waited in huddles for tables to be cleared and their names to be called; a basketball game played on the television over the bar; servers hustled steaming plates through the flapping door between kitchen and dining room; the sky darkened over the snow and sidewalks, leafless tree limbs, and distant open water.

My husband, son, and I sat at a table by the window, but the only light came from candles and dim track lighting along the ceiling. Looking up and over and behind, I saw hanging on the restaurant's walls dozens and dozens of framed black-and-white, eight-by-ten photographs. I searched among them for a recognizable face. These were not the celebrity photographs common on this city's restaurant walls: the owner with his arm draped across the mayor's shoulder; the owner beaming in a handgrip with a former U.S. president; the owner with Tony Bennett or Barbra Streisand, with Michael Jordan, Mike Ditka, or Sammy Sosa. Where was a face from the newspaper, television, or the movies?

Everywhere, portrait shots. A young woman with long blond hair; another with a brunette bob; others with barrettes and ponytails, braids, Farrah Fawcett wings, afros, curly perms, pixie cuts, clips, and headbands. The young women wore wool sweaters, peasant blouses, and halter-tops. They sat on park swings and rocks or leaned against trees. There were only a scattering of young men.

"Who are these people on the walls?" I asked our waitress, her dark hair cut short, framing a round face, dark bright eyes, and welcoming smile.

"Waiters and waitresses who've worked here," she said. "Everyone gets their picture taken and hung."

I asked where her picture was.

"Just around that corner," she said with a gesture over her shoulder. "Above the first booth on the left."

Mystery solved, and we returned to our eating. We talked, laughed, and took our time. Maybe we'd see a movie afterward, and so we opened the newspaper to look for theater times. Later, I looked for the waitress's picture.

And there it was. "Sometimes they get pretty beat up," the salesclerk told me as he turned Mary this way and that like a grocery shopper inspecting a melon. He found what he was looking for and pointed to a scuffed indentation on the underside of the top right corner. His assistant nodded and wrote something on a clipboard. The salesclerk told me that this icon and the others still in the box had actually hung in a church somewhere, which meant they had been kissed, bowed to, and saturated in incense, not just punched out of a factory for religious trinkets.

"How much?" I asked out of curiosity. He responded with a four-figure number somewhere between the cost of my monthly mortgage payment and a used car.

He lifted a second icon from the box, again encased in an *oklad*. About 50 percent bigger than the first, this icon—of Jesus—carried nearly twice the price tag. His face appeared through a window in the silver, as did another smaller figure, also Jesus, standing on the left side and no taller than the span of a hand. On the right side stood an equally small Mary, her face also open at a window.

"Where had they hung?" I asked. He didn't know. But what he did know was this: when icons are removed from a church, they must be de-sacralized; if they are ever returned, they must be re-sacralized.

I asked him what that meant, imagining some mysterious back-room ritual involving water and fire. He shook his head and shrugged.

Not knowing the ways of the East, I come from a world away: Scandinavian pietism through the prism of American Protestantism, or perhaps the other way around. But the stories the icons represent transcend those differences. Fifty-four Byzantine icons hang in the museum gallery adjacent to and on the floor below the gift shop. Painted in the seventeenth and eighteenth centuries, these icons survived despite being seized by the new Soviet regime. Some had been found years later, buried in an attic. Most are as tall and wide as a movie poster. Each icon has a wood panel layered with a linen cloth, gesso (a mixture of chalk and glue), strategically placed gold leaf, and glazed tempera paint (mineral pigments mixed with egg yolk and water) primarily in warm hues—emerald green, crimson, cinnabar. According to an information plaque on the wall, the presence of gold leaf signifies "a sanctified state."

Against the south wall of the ground-level nave, prison chains break at Peter's feet, and Simeon, his curls etched in gold, holds Mary's baby. On the west wall within a semicircular apse, John the Baptist's head is on a golden pedestal platter and ravens feed Elijah in the desert. Mary hangs above, never without her baby.

Around the corner to the right stands Michael the Archangel, stately in deacon's garb of red and gold, wings on his back and a mirror in his hand through which he and Jesus talk.

Glancing up from the ground-level nave, I see the icons lining the mezzanine's walls. Gold disc halos glimmer everywhere. Up the stairs, there hangs another Mary, her head wrapped in a headscarf studded with pearls, and Adam and Eve grab a helping hand out of hell. Joseph sits dejected in a cave, his head slumped into his open palm.

In the "Feasts Tier," a row of 10 icons, the "Transfiguration of our Lord" hangs second from the end. Jesus takes center position with a robe as white as light, a sash of gold, Moses and Elijah to his right and left, respectively. Gold halos on each. Unlike all the other icons in this exhibit, this one shows movement. Their robes and capes furl as the three men hover above ground in imagined wind. Hands and arms with bent elbows are caught mid-motion, a conversation clearly in progress. As the story goes, Jesus's face glows like the sun, but I don't see it here. A layer of cotton-ball clouds hold the icon's browns, greens, yellows, and reds down to earth, as if in shadow, the background above nothing but creamy white, the clouds just gray enough to suggest a degree of threat. Has the benedictory voice already spoken? On the hard ground—which yet managed to bloom a flowering plant and sprout a sapling—looking this way and that, twist the fearful Peter, James, and John.

Ashley, Brittany, and Nick walk in the Chicago restaurant's door as new hires, and Cindy, Laura, and Bob under glass have no choice but to reposition. Someone pushes aside a table or two, pulls the ladder from the storeroom, props it against the wall, and climbs.

This restaurant has been in business for more than three decades. The total number of possible portraits could easily pass 1,000, but no doubt some servers decline to have their pictures taken or displayed, and some pictures have been damaged over the years, glass breaking of idiopathic causation or the framed unit slipping off a nail and crashing down.

Still, room must be made for more. Perhaps the climber will swoosh a dust cloth around the glass of the surrounding others at the same time. Wipe off splatters of ketchup, barbecue sauce, and chili with a wet rag. Do it unto the least of these, said Mary's baby all grown up.

Shift up, down; shift left, right. A space opens and a new face is lifted up. The hand painted by Michelangelo that reached across the Sistine Chapel's dome pointed here and life sparked.

God sees, say the icons. Among the objects of his gaze are surely these three-dimensional servers in two-dimensional portrait on the wall. The creator's created, all in the order of Adam and Eve, of Michelangelo and Gaudí, of store clerks and healers.

Scientist and priest Pavel Florensky was imprisoned in a Siberian labor camp in 1933. I've been reading his seminal book about icons. Lincoln famously said that every person over 40 is responsible for his own face, but Florensky suggests an increment of complication. "A face is the perceptual raw material upon which the portrait-artist is now working," he wrote, "but whose esthetic details are, at the moment, still unfinished." For Florensky, a face was a mask unless transfigured into a countenance, and with such a view, he jumps into the very nature of being. Let us make human beings in our image, said the triune Godhead, and the seed of countenance passes.

I think long and hard about this, and all the while candlelight reflects off the framed portraits on the restaurant walls, courting, wooing, daring ancient countenance to emerge, loaning some of its flicker and shine, the grace of original light. For my sons I often pray the ancient benediction: *"The Lord bless you and keep you."* If the reality of color could push up through those black-and-white prints, taking our eyes from the speckle of flat-yellow mustard splashes on the glass, then gold chains around necks would sparkle. *"The Lord make his face to shine upon you and be gracious to you."* Gold bands encircling fingers and gold hoops dangling from ears would flash. *"The Lord lift up his countenance upon you and give you peace."*

On a day yet to come, my husband will be dropping me off at the airport for a work trip, and as we pull up to the curb, he will tell me. He didn't get the latest job for which he had applied, interviewed, and been high in the running; the job that we had prayed for, thought of as the light at the end of the tunnel, and already regarded as the turning point. We will barely speak but instead face each other and look eye to eye: a kiss, a hug, the drive home for him, the walk through the airport for me. *The Lord lift up his countenance upon you, and give you peace.*

"Gold," wrote Florensky, "is one of the most conclusive proofs that icon painting possesses a concretely metaphysical meaning." Paint and gold side by side on a wooden panel, light bouncing off the first but penetrating the other, its luster dazzling, makes it plain to see that "wholly different spheres of existence" are before our very eyes.

Outside the museum, above this neighborhood of church bells, coffee shops and markets, the planes fly low overhead. Here in this neighborhood, in this area under the curve, in this mysterious metaphysical God-filled universe is where I live and work. Here, I make and find my livelihood. Road construction and traffic on the adjacent highway pound and hum. Shovels scrape; computer keys click; birds call. This is the soundtrack for the milieu where labor and grace commune.

Time to choose the gift, and so I left the salesclerk at his work. He slid a ladder against a dark wood bookcase and climbed up. He lifted then lowered the two icons, one at a time, onto their respective nails on the white wall. The ordinary and extraordinary slip and slide past each other while the clock ticks.

Florensky wrote that art can't be made on the way to spiritual experience—on the ascent—but only on the way down. What's true for art is true for life. I think of the mountain of the Transfiguration where heaven and earth are of one piece. Here is the moment humanity strains for, longs for. Anticipation is quenched, epiphany not just a swell of emotion or intellect but a wave of sublime reality. The moment passes though. Jesus and his friends go down the mountain, and he says, Don't tell. Life goes on with the moment hidden inside. Things the same; things never the same.

Satisfied, I finished my tea as a second salesclerk wrapped the gift in tissue and placed it in a box. A lacquered broach—spray of red, blue, and yellow flowers against a black background—signed by the artist on the back in gold.

I returned to work to begin again. Breath and blood, flesh and brain, heart and bones. The weeks are holy.

Final Word

A CHALLENGE AND A BENEDICTION

Thank you, dear reader, for reading this book. Let me now send you off with a challenge and a benediction.

~

THE CHALLENGE

Consider your own experiences of work, no matter whether your work falls short of or far exceeds what you thought you'd do in this life. You are at once worker, witness, and narrator, protagonist and minor character. Write your experiences. Aim for 20 stories, images, or people that fill a place of permanence in your memory. Fill a notebook, a stack of index cards, or an electronic file. Scribble in the margins your longings and disappointments, your passion and needs, your aspirations and limits, the tension of your planned life and your given life.

Arrange whatever pieces come your way. Disentangle the essentials from the messy knots of real life; waste nothing; call on it all.

Reorder until the click of yes, this is how you make your case; this is how the meaning emerges.

Take a long, contemplative look. What can you discover about life and your place in it, about the flow of love and grace moving in you and through you? Open your eyes wide and see; shut them and think. You're aiming for glimpses of what's really going on here: how work becomes more than what it is and how you become who you're meant to be in the process; how you find livelihood even as you are making it.

Share your experiences with someone. Share your questions and conclusions. Share them with me. I'd love to hear from you.

~

The Benediction

May you have livelihood in the fullest sense of the word.

May your eyes be opened to the larger transcendent reality that enfolds your work.

May you live and work in the flow of God's love and grace, to you and through you.

May your work be absorbed into the overall spiritual journey that is your life.

May your longing for meaning be satisfied even when your daily work fails to satisfy.

May you be refreshed in the time and space of Sabbath-like leisure.

May we all make peace with the shadows.

Acknowledgments

I have many people to thank.

The Kalos Press team: Ed Eubanks for his leadership, which made everything possible; Jessica Snell, for skillfully and gracefully steering this book to completion; Jenni Simmons, for saying yes; Beth Hart, for her careful eye and editorial good sense; Deborah Ferguson and Laura Kwiatkowski, for their superlative proofreading; Valerie Anne Bost, for her design artistry, which made this book a thing of beauty.

Lisa Ohlen Harris, Jill Noel Kandel, and Karen Miedrich-Luo: for the gift of a virtual writers group, generous with motivational pushes and cheers, editorial critique, and wise perspective. Nancy Cripe: for walking along with me through pages of this book, as a writer and a friend. Linda Solie and Tim and Cyd Johnson: for reading an in-progress version of this manuscript and giving me valuable feedback and encouragement. Jessica Brown: for catching the vision for this book and helping me hold on to it, and for her gentle and insightful reading of an earlier draft. Laurie Harper and Katie Nordenson: for specific professional editorial counsel.

My Seattle Pacific University cohort, including Jessica Brown, Ann Conway, Karin Evans, Matt Gallant, Chad Gusler, Rebecca

Kasparek, George Linn, Kelly Foster Lundquist, Margaret Sefton, Amie Sharp, Mary Van Denend, and Brian Volck: for feedback to early writing of some sections of this book and for precious and ongoing camaraderie in this writing life. Greg Wolfe, Leslie Leyland Fields, and Robert Clark: for teaching me so much. The Collegeville Institute and the Lilly Endowment: for facilitating space and time for writing during summer writing workshops.

Janet and John Erickson, my parents, to whom this book is dedicated: for their constant love and encouragement. Erick, Katie, Alex, and Katherine, my sons and daughters-in-law: for filling my life with love, beauty, and joy. Dave, my husband: for being my first and best reader; for the haven of his love, wisdom, and humor; for his unwavering support of this project.

Praise God from whom all blessings flow.

Notes

Book and Act Epigraphs

"What is a Progress. . .leading to Revelation?": Fanny Howe, *The Winter Sun: Notes on a Vocation* (Saint Paul, Minn.: Graywolf Press, 2009), 129.

"Is there still an arena of human action. . .a 'five-year plan'?": Josef Pieper, *Leisure: The Basis of Culture*, trans. Gerald Malsbary (South Bend, Ind.: St. Augustine's Press, 1998), 22.

"Jobs are not big enough for people. . .you know?": Nora Watson in Studs Terkel, *Working: People Talk About What They Do All Day and How They Feel About What They Do* (New York: Ballantine, 1985), 675.

"Six days a week the spirit is alone. . .waiting for man to join it.": Abraham Joshua Heschel, *The Sabbath: Its Meaning for Modern Man* (New York: Farrar, Straus and Giroux, 2005), 65.

"Oh God. . .this double thread of my life.": Pierre Teilhard de Chardin. *The Divine Milieu; An Essay on the Interior Life* (New York: Harper, 1965), 80.

Prologue

"It's a hard feeling. . .but not to talk to you.": Heather Lamb in Terkel, *Working*, 69.

"What I do. . .five people.": Therese Carter in Ibid., 398.

"When your work sheet. . .just your number.": Steve Dubi in Ibid., 716.

"It is about a search… a Monday through Friday sort of dying.": Ibid., xiii.

Livelihood…In the fullest sense of the word: Based on *Oxford English Dictionary*, 3rd ed., s.v. "livelihood," definitions 1, 2, and 3.

Philosophers and theologians…the means to leisure: For a discussion of these theories of work, see Gilbert Meilaender, *Working: Its Meaning and Its Limits* (Notre Dame, Ind: University of Notre Dame Press, 2000).

"the place God calls you…the world's deep hunger meet.": Frederick Buechner, *Wishful Thinking: A Theological ABC* (New York: Harper & Row, 1973), 95.

a sentiment first voiced by Aristotle: The quote attributed to Aristotle is, "Where your talents and the needs of the world cross, there lies your vocation."

Travels in Sunshine City

"penman": Oxford English Dictionary, 3rd ed., s.v. "penman," definitions 1a and 2.

"How do you expect to arrive…road to another man's city?": Thomas Merton, *New Seeds of Contemplation* (New York: New Directions Book, 2007), 100.

Case Study

"The most important lesson…a malarial parasite.": Richard Cabot, *Case Teaching in Medicine* (Boston: D. C. Heath & Co, 1907), vii.

"After the student has learned…shut them and think.": Ibid., vii.

"Then we can help the student to disentangle the essentials": Ibid.

"Arrange whatever pieces come your way.": Virginia Woolf, *A Writer's Diary*, ed. Leonard Woolf (New York: Harcourt Brace & Company, 1981), 80.

"signal of transcendence": Peter L. Berger, *A Rumor of Angels: Modern Society and the Rediscovery of the Supernatural* (Garden City, NJ: Anchor Books, 1970), 54.

Gestures of play and hope are such signals too, he wrote: Berger, *A Rumor of Angels*, 52–60.

Once I read a paper…an airplane being readied for flight: Moises Auron-Gomez and Franklin Michota, "Medical management of hip fracture," *Clinics in Geriatric Medicine* 24, no. 4 (November 2008), 702.

SUMMA LABORUM I

"a summarized debate…a shared journey of discovery.": Peter Kreeft in Saint Thomas Aquinas and Peter Kreeft, *A Shorter Summa: The Most Essential Philosophical Passages of St. Thomas Aquinas' Summa Theologica* (San Francisco: Ignatius Press, 1993), 17.

Each article in the Summa *has five parts*: Ibid., 20–21.

"Why Work?": See Dorothy L. Sayers, "Why Work?" in Sayers, *Creed or Chaos* (London, Methuen & Co. Ltd, 1947), 47–64.

"the place God calls you…world's deep hunger meet.": Buechner, *Wishful Thinking*, 95.

Agrarians, artisans, and craftsmen write of the satisfaction: For example, see Brian Keeble, *God and Work: Aspects of Art and Tradition* (Bloomington, Ind.: World Wisdom, Inc., 2009).

"My eyes are almost bleeding.": Gerard Manley Hopkins, *Gerard Manley Hopkins: The Major Works*, ed. Catherine Phillips (New York: Oxford University Press, 2002), 271.

METRICS

"Calculative thought places itself…the unforeseeable coming of the ineluctable.": Martin Heidegger, *Existence and Being*, ed. Werner Brock (London: Vision Press, 1956), 388, 391.

The sublime as per Longinus: See Longinus, On "The Sublime," trans. W. H. Fyfe in *Aristotle: Poetics; Longinus: On the Sublime; Demetrius: On Style* (Cambridge, Mass: Harvard University Press, 2005), 173.

First Author, et Al., ad Infinitum

"My hand made an instrument...He Himself shall hearken.": *The Psalter* (Boston: Holy Transfiguration Monastery, 2007), 226.

The 10th edition of the American Medical Association Manual of Style states... "disagreement about order should be resolved by the authors, not the editor.": American Medical Association, *AMA Manual of Style*, 10th ed. (New York: Oxford University Press, 2007),134.

"My heart is not proud.": Psalms 131:1–3, NIV.

Breath and Blood

"My respiration and inspiration...through my lungs": Walt Whitman, "Song of Myself" in Whitman, *The Works of Walt Whitman* (Ware, Hertfordshire: Wordsworth, 2006), 24.

Chinese medicine takes no pulse...every 300 or so breaths: See Shigehisa Kuriyama, *The Expressiveness of the Body and the Divergence of Greek and Chinese Medicine* (New York, NY: Zone Books, 2002), 17–60.

Still in French Airspace

Rainer Maria Rilke wrote Stories Of God...Pass the stories along to the children, he said: Rainer Maria Rilke, *Stories of God*, trans. M. D. Herter Norton (New York: W. W. Norton & Company, Inc., 1963), 10, 17–19, 80, 115.

In the book's first story: Ibid., 17–27.

"in such a hurry to live": Ibid., 23.

"distorted people's faces badly.": Ibid., 24.

"pierce the canopy" Pieper, *Leisure,* 69.

transcend the "work-a-day world": Ibid., 67.

"the totality of existing things to come into play: God and the World": Ibid., 97.

To be human: Pieper makes this point throughout *Leisure.*

"a condition of the soul.": Pieper, *Leisure,* 30.

"Joy is play's intention": Berger, *A Rumor of Angels,* 58.

"how that spear joins heaven and earth.": Juan Eduardo Cirlot, Pere Vivas, and Ricard Pla, *Gaudí: An Introduction to His Architecture* (Menorca, Spain; Triangle Postals, 2001), 170.

"And I will put breath in you. . .and you will come to life.": Ezekiel 37:6, NIV.

In C. S. Lewis's The Last Battle, *there is a scene*: C. S. Lewis, *The Last Battle* (New York; HarperTrophy, 1994), 180–81.

"the whole order of real things be registered in our soul": Pieper, *Leisure,* 79.

"What is that in your hand?": Exodus 4:2, NIV.

WITNESS

"Eyes see better when guided by love.": Josef Pieper, *Only the Lover Sings: Art and Contemplation,* trans. Lothar Krauth (San Francisco: Ignatius Press, 1990), 74.

TWO-PART INVENTION

"But do your work, and I shall know you.": Ralph Waldo Emerson, "Self-Reliance" in Emerson, *Essays & Poems* (New York: Library of America College Editions, 1996), 264.

"a plain Method of learning. . .how to develop the same well.": Johann Sebastian Bach, *Fifteen Two-Part Inventions* (New York: G. Schirmer, Inc., 1894), 3.

"Do your work, and you shall reinforce yourself.": Emerson, *Essays & Poems,* 264.

Poet and essayist Adam Zagajewski tells the story...before landing on the concept of metaxu: Adam Zagajewski, *A Defense of Ardor*, trans. Clare Cavanagh (New York: Farrar, Straus, and Giroux, 2005), 5–11.

"We see. . .almost as a disk.": National Aeronautics and Space Administration (NASA), "Apollo 8: Day 1: The Green Team and Separation" in Apollo Flight Journal, http://history.nasa.gov/ap08fj /03day1_green_sep.htm.

"a beholding that ascends.": Pavel Florensky, *Iconostasis,* trans. Donald Sheehan and Olga Andrejev (Crestwood, NY: St. Vladimir's Seminary Press, 2000), 72.

advice by the unknown author of The Cloud of Unknowing. . .*impressions to the contrary:* Anonymous, *The Cloud of Unknowing,* ed. William Johnston (New York: Image Books, 1996), 56.

Julian of Norwich saw in a hazelnut all that was ever made: Julian of Norwich, *The Shewings of Julian of Norwich,* lines 148–51, http://d.lib.rochester.edu /teams/text/the-shewings-of-julian-of-norwich-part-1.

There is Elijah. . .He lives: I Kings 17.

May the LORD *make him to live:* I Kings 17:21.

BREAK

"Coffee. . .word of the Lord is to the soul.": Isak Dinesen, "The Supper at Elsinore" in *Seven Gothic Tales* (New York; Vintage International, 1991), 245.

Lake Superior. . .that it has swallowed more than 350 ships: Visit Duluth. "Lake Superior Facts," http://www.visitduluth.com/about /lake_superior_facts.php.

"Does any one know. . .minutes to hours?": Gordon Lightfoot, "Wreck of the Edmund Fitzgerald," 1975, http://gordonlightfoot.com /wreckoftheedmundfitzgerald.shtml.

"I have made this object with my hands. . .between maker and user.": Kent McLaughlin, Artist Statement.

"*Time for you and time for me. . .Before the taking of a toast and tea.*": T. S. Eliot, "The Love Song of J Alfred Prufrock," 1920, http://www.bartleby.com /198/1.html.

I have been listening to an online audio meditation. . .the meditation today: Jesuits in Britain, Pray As You Go, March 30, 2006, http://pray-as-you-go.org /prayer/?uid=758.

Away We Go

Robert Richardson's biography. . .a quote from Goethe, "To live within limits, to want one thing. . .": Goethe in Robert D. Richardson, *Henry Thoreau: A Life of the Mind* (University of California Press, 1986).

Summa Laborum II

I am drawn to the story of Albert Schweitzer. . .where he was often paid with bananas or eggs: Albert Schweitzer, *Out of My Life and Thought: An Autobiography* (New York: H. Holt, 1991), 82, 86, 140.

I am drawn to the story of John the Baptist. . .wild honey: Matthew 3:4.

Josef Pieper might say. . .to fulfill a social function Pieper, Leisure, 42, 45-47.

"Vocation is responsibility. . .to the whole of reality.": Dietrich Bonhoeffer, "Vocation" in *Ethics*, ed. Eberhard Bethge (New York: The Macmillan Company, 1955) 225–26.

"This life. . .responsibility.": Ibid., 223.

For Bonhoeffer. . .horizontally to people and things: Ibid., 225.

A Place at the Table

A theophany on a mountaintop and Moses came back glowing: Exodus 33:18-23, Exodus 34:29.

"In a colorful career…walls of an inner world.": Lawry O'Day, Soliloquys (sic) About Special Occasions, unpublished.

"The hapless ways of destiny…broken wing.": Ibid.

"In the realm of suffering…its own particular mark": Simone Weil, Waiting for God (New York: Harper, 1973), 117.

"that has seized…social, psychological, and physical.": Ibid., 119.

"Thou art indeed just…so what I plead is just.": Hopkins, "Justus quidem tu es, Domine" in Gerard Manley Hopkins: The Major Works, 183.

"is a nail whose point is applied at the very center of the soul.": Weil, Waiting for God, 134–35.

"divine technique…a simple and ingenious device.": Ibid., 135.

the image of a butterfly pinned alive into an album: Ibid., 135.

"He whose soul remains…separating the soul from God.": Ibid., 135.

"But thou art making me…though my brain should reel.": George MacDonald, Diary of an Old Soul (Minneapolis, Minn: Augsburg Fortress, 1994), 100.

SPINNING AND BEING SPUN

"And what does the Lord require of you? To act justly and to love mercy and to walk humbly with your God.": Micah 6:8, NIV.

"Elsewhere the sky is the roof of the world…was the sky, the sky!": Willa Cather, Death Comes for the Archbishop (New York: Vintage Books, 1990), 232.

By the sweat of your brow you will eat your food: Genesis 3:19, NIV.

What is in your hand?: Exodus 4:2.

Establish Thou the work of our hands: Psalms 90:17, KJV.

Who knows but you have been placed here for such a time as this?: Esther 4:14

Once these signs have been fulfilled, whatever your hands find to do, do it: I Samuel 10:7

Work to live.: Aristotle. *Nicomachean Ethics* X, 7 (1177b4-6), trans. Martin Ostwald. (Upper Saddle River, NJ: Library of Liberal Arts, 1999), 289.

Let it be to me as you have said.: Luke 1:38.

If it be thy will, let this cup pass from me.: Matthew 26:39.

Painting is not my trade!: Michelangelo. *I, Michelangelo, Sculptor: An Autobiogrphay Through Letters*, ed. Irving Stone and Jean Stone, trans. Charles Speroni (Garden City, NY: Doubleday & Co, Inc, 1962), 42.

...obedience...: Weil, *Waiting for God*, 63.

"One paints what is around": Georgia O'Keeffe, from a display at the Georgia O'Keeffe Museum in Santa Fe, New Mexico, 2005.

"There is no need to bother about what has been told to others; there are words for you alone.": Jean-Pierre de Caussade, *The Sacrament of the Present Moment*, trans. Kitty Muggeridge (New York, NY: HarperSanFrancisco, 1982), 73.

"All we need to know is how to recognize his will in the present moment.": de Caussade, *Sacrament of the Present Moment*, 43.

To paraphrase de Caussade: calm, calm; there is a hiding place where silk is spun in secret: de Caussade, *Sacrament of the Present Moment*, 40.

"Everything leads...air and water are made divine.": de Caussade, *Sacrament of the Present Moment*, 72.

SUMMA LABORUM III

Antiquity: when the leisure...vocation and capitalism went hand in hand: For an overview of historical thought on work and vocation, see William C. Placher, *Callings: Twenty Centuries of Christian Wisdom on Vocation* (Grand Rapids, Mich: W.B. Eerdmans Pub. Co, 2005).

charisms be employed: For a discussion of a theology of work based on charisms, see Miroslav Volf, *Work in the Spirit: Toward a Theology of Work* (Eugene, Ore: Wipf and Stock, 2001).

another contingent holds...paired to life as a whole: For example, see Gilbert Meilaender, "Friendship and Vocation" in *Friendship, a Study in Theological Ethics* (Notre Dame, Ind: University of Notre Dame Press, 1981), 86–103. Also, Gilbert Meilaender, *The Freedom of a Christian: Grace, Vocation, and the Meaning of Our Humanity* (Grand Rapids, Mich: Brazos Press, 2006).

Buechner famously ruled out...the worker is bored: Buechner, *Wishful Thinking*, 95.

"Remain in my love...one's life for one's friends.": John 15: 9–13, NAB.

Let it be to me as you have said: Luke 1:38.

when Samuel..."Here I am": I Samuel 3.

when Jesus...leave their nets: Mark 1:17–18 and Matthew 4:19–20.

Add the word "subject," a...in her memoir of vocation: Howe, *The Winter Sun*, 22, 89, 94, 107.

Write the words "inscape" and "instress," and...as action of the mind or will: See Christopher Devlin's commentary on Hopkin's use of these words in Gerard Manley Hopkins, *The Sermons and Devotional Writings of Gerard Manley Hopkins*, ed. Christopher Devlin (Oxford University Press, 1967) 109, 283–84, 293.

ONE THOUSAND AND ONE TALES OF NOW

thanks to a paper published...of the double-helix structure of DNA: James D. Watson, Francis H. Crick, "Molecular Structure of Nucleic Acids: A Structure for Deoxyribose Nucleic Acid," in *Nature* 171, no. 4356 (April 25, 1953), 737-38.

"Your years are as...In you today is eternity": Saint Augustine, Bishop of Hippo. *Confessions: Books I-XIII*, trans. by F. J. Sheed (Indianapolis, Ind: Hackett Pub. Co, 1993), 219.

CENTRIPETAL CENTRIFUGAL COUNTERPOISE

"Our souls can only be...What more can we ask?": deCaussade, *Sacrament of the Present Moment*, 81.

"Go out into the darkness...safer than a known way.": Minnie Louise Haskins, "God Knows" (also called "The Gate of the Year") in *The Desert*, 1908.

"What do people get from...their minds do not rest.": Ecclesiastes 2:22–23, NIV.

"Blessed are those...set on pilgrimage": Psalms 84:5, NIV.

Hope...beyond reality: Berger, *A Rumor of Angels*, 53, 60.

Simone Weil wrote of a center... arms of the cross: Weil, *Waiting for God*, 135–136.

I'm practicing not glossing over...Psalms now and again in the Orthodox version I sometimes read, "So be it.": *The Psalter*, 66, 110, 139, 166.

BODY OF WORK

As God challenged...Can these bones live?: Ezekiel 37:3.

the project director borrowed words..."We go from strength to strength.": Psalms 84:7.

PHYSIOLOGY LESSONS

"Pray to remember...power of the Spirit.": Edward Hays, *The Pilgrimage Way of the Cross* (Leavenworth, Kansas: Forest of Peace Pub, 2003), 39.

"dedicate with faith...God's liberation of the world.": Ibid., 43.

He imagines that in some sort of time warp...Why sleep ye?: Georges Bernanos, *The Diary of a Country Priest*, trans. Pamela Morris (London: Fount, 1977), 159.

Bernanos's troubled young priest...agony of Gethsemane: Ibid., 160.

"Every action, seen through God's eyes...to the infinite.": Massimo Camisasca, "Light of the World" in *Magnificat* 6, no. 13 (February 2005), 92.

There's an ancient story...to set the offering ablaze: Judges 6.

"Go in the strength you have." Judges 6:14, NIV.

"And what you thought you came for. . .If at all.": T. S. Eliot, *Four Quarters* (San Diego: Harcourt, 1971), 50.

Frisson evoked by music. . .from that evoked by fear: David Huron, *Sweet Anticipation: Music and The Psychology of Expectation* (Cambridge, Mass: MIT Press, 2007), 34.

PORTRAIT GALLERY

their current exhibit, "Transcendent Art: Icons from Yaroslavl, Russia": The Museum of Russian Art, "Transcendent Art: Icons from Yaroslavl, Russia," September 22, 2008 – January 24, 2009.

"A face is the perceptual raw material. . .still unfinished.": Florensky, *Iconostasis,* 51.

For Florensky, a face was a mask unless transfigured into a countenance: Ibid., 50–53.

Let us make. . .in our own image: Genesis 1:26.

"The Lord bless you and keep you. . .give you peace.": Numbers 6:24-26, ESV.

"Gold. . .a concretely metaphysical meaning.": Florensky, *Iconostasis,* 120.

"wholly different spheres of existence": Ibid., 123.

Florensky wrote that art. . .but only on the way down: Ibid., 44–45.

I think of the mountain of the Transfiguration. . .and he says, Don't tell: Matthew 17:1–9, Mark 9:2–9, Luke 9:28–36.

FINAL WORD

Arrange whatever pieces come your way.: Woolf, *A Writer's Diary,* 80.

Author's Note

I have changed the names and identifying characteristics of some people, projects, and institutions.

About the Author

Nancy J. Nordenson is a nationally recognized author and essayist. Her writing has appeared in *Harvard Divinity Bulletin, Indiana Review, Comment, Under the Sun, Relief,* and in other publications and anthologies, including *The Spirit of Food: 34 Writers on Feasting and Fasting Toward God* (Cascade), *Becoming: What Makes a Woman* (University of Nebraska Gender Studies), and *Not Alone: A Literary and Spiritual Companion for those Confronted with Infertility and Miscarriage* (Kalos Press). Her work has also earned multiple "notable" recognitions in the *Best American Essays* and *Best Spiritual Writing* anthologies, and Pushcart Prize nominations. Her first book, *Just Think: Nourish Your Mind to Feed Your Soul* was published by Baker Books.

By day, Nancy earns her living as a freelance medical writer and has written for a variety of venues, including continuing medical education programs and national and international medical symposia. She is also an accredited medical technologist and has worked as a laboratory consultant and educator. Nancy graduated from North Park University in Chicago with a BA in biology and chemistry and earned an MFA in creative writing from Seattle

Pacific University. Nancy and her husband, Dave, live in Minneapolis and have two married sons.

For more information, visit www.nancynordenson.com and www.findinglivelihood.com.

About Kalos Press

Kalos Press was established to give a voice to literary fiction, memoir, essays, poetry, devotional writing, and Christian reflection—works of excellent quality, outside of the mainstream Christian publishing industry.

We believe that good writing is beautiful in form and in function, and is capable of being an instrument of transformation. It is our hope and ambition that every title produced by Kalos Press will live up to this belief.

For more information about Kalos Press, *Finding Livelihood,* and/or our other titles, or for ordering information, visit us on our website: www.kalospress.org, or contact us by e-mail at info@kalospress.org.

Finding Livelihood— *Digital*

At Kalos Press, we've found that we often appreciate owning both print and digital editions of the books we read; perhaps you have found this as well. In our gratitude to you for purchasing a print version of this book, we are pleased to offer you free copies of the digital editions of *Finding Livelihood*. To obtain one or more of these, simply visit the eStore of our parent ministry, Doulos Resources (estore.doulosresources.org) and enter the following discount code during checkout:

DigitalLivelihood

If you purchased a digital edition, you may use the same discount code to receive a discount deducting the full price of your digital edition off of the purchase price for a print edition.

Thank you for your support!

CPSIA information can be obtained
at www.ICGtesting.com
Printed in the USA
FFOW03n1501020515